To Tara,

Thank you —

Mary Ellen Nordyke Grace

Robert A. Nordyke, M.D.

I'M THIRD

God is First,

Everyone Else is Second,

I'm Third

AN AMERICAN BOY

of

DEPRESSION YEARS

Memoirs of

ROBERT A. NORDYKE, M.D.

EDITED BY

Eleanor C. Nordyke

Aimee M. Grace

About the Editors

ELEANOR C. NORDYKE, wife of Robert A. Nordyke, M.D., has resided in
Honolulu, Hawai'i since she was four years old. She attended Punahou School
(class of 1945), received a B.S. from Stanford University, a public health nursing
certificate from the University of California at Berkeley, and a M.P.H. from the
University of Hawai'i. As a research fellow at the East-West Center, she was a specialist in the population of Hawai'i, writing numerous demographic publications,
including *The Peopling of Hawai'i* (1977 and 1989). She is the author, in collaboration with James A. Mattison, Jr., M.D., of *Pacific Images, Views from Captain
Cook's Third Voyage* (1999).

AIMEE M. GRACE, granddaughter of Robert A. Nordyke, M.D., was born and
raised in Honolulu, Hawai'i, graduated from Punahou School (class of 2000), and
attends Stanford University. She shared many experiences with her grandfather,
sat on his lap to listen to his bedtime tales of growing up in California during
the Depression years of the 1920's and 1930's, memorized his favorite poems,
and assisted in planning and typing this book.

✧ ✧ ✧

ISBN 1-883528-26-7

On the cover and page ii: Robert A. Nordyke in front of Sather Gate
      at UC Berkeley, 1938.
Page 97: Verse "All that you gave, you have," is taken from *To Hattie Belle Ege*,
      by E. O. James, Professor of English, Mills College, Oakland, California, 1913.

Illustrations in this book are from the Nordyke family collection
unless otherwise noted and are used with permission.

Page 35: Willys-Knight automobile,
      <www.1inamillioncars.com/29willys8.jpg>
Page 46: Barber dime, <www.oldcoinshop.com/coinhistory/10c-1892-1916.htm>
Page 80: Freight train in San Francisco railyard,
      <freespace.virgin.net/andrew.halling/trains/trains.html>
Page 122: Piper Cub, Lockheed Lodestar, and Boeing B-17G airplanes,
      <www.wpafb.af.mil/museum/air_power/ap16.htm>
Page 134: Cars on San Francisco Bay Bridge,
      <http://www.americahurrah.com/SanFrancisco/The40s/bridgeEB.jpg>

Designed and produced by Barbara Pope Book Design
Printed in China

CONTENTS

The Robert A. Nordyke family at Stanford University, 1967.

FOREWORD

My father, Robert A. Nordyke, was a prominent physician in Honolulu, Hawai'i, for almost forty years. He was highly respected by his fellow physicians for his expertise in the field of nuclear medicine and for his special interest in diseases of the thyroid gland. His regular patients loved him for his general medical skills and caring nature.

Dad passed away in 1997 at the age of 78, but the bow wave of his passage through life has left a very positive impact on our Honolulu community as well as all those who ever knew him. The Pacific Health Research Institute and Straub Foundation, important local medical research entities, were initiated, in large part, by my father's efforts, and they continue to support various clinical research projects. His long-term association with the University of Hawai'i's John A. Burns School of Medicine as a clinical professor allowed him to mentor and mold hundreds of aspiring physicians in training who are now in active practice in the United States and throughout the Pacific region. I, as a physician in the Hawai'i Kai area of Honolulu with a busy internal medicine practice, often feel myself bobbing in my father's wake when I receive unsolicited referrals from physicians who knew my father and suspect that some of his personal and professional qualities may somehow have splashed onto his son. I am also privileged to care for many people who still complain fervently and regretfully about receiving a personalized letter of farewell from my father when he felt it necessary to withdraw from active clinical practice in 1995.

Of course, to me, as I was growing up, my father was just my father—irrespective of his broad professional demands and accomplishments. He was a very busy person, but he made a special effort to arrive home by six o'clock in the evening to join the family at dinner, and my four sisters and I could count on him to advise us with our homework, to tuck us into bed, and to spend a good part of an hour just talking. Sometimes he would tell us about the activities of the day; sometimes he would recite several of the many favorite poems he knew by heart. But, often, he would tell us stories of his childhood. These stories were especially popular because of their intrinsic entertainment value and his wonderful sense of humor. We came to know the stories well and would request our favorites to be told and retold—always with additional facts and detail. The poems were fine, but the stories were best.

Those evening story-telling sessions helped to bond my sisters and me more closely to my father. They also provided us with a better understanding of the Depression years and how that era, although materially difficult, helped to formulate and solidify his moral character. His interest in supporting and caring for his fellow man eclipsed any desire to accumulate wealth.

It is fortunate that my father, in his later years, placed pen to paper and recorded many of the same stories that my sisters and I enjoyed as bedtime entertainment. In addition to his skills as a physician, he also had an excellent command of the English language and was able to imbue these stories with clarity and wit. It is also fortunate that his wife, my mother, has had the energy and emotional fortitude to pore through these documents, with many a tear in her eye I'm sure, and bring together this very special compendium of recollections. I hope that, as you read these stories, you will catch a glimpse of the life of an American boy during the Depression years and come to understand, in some small way, the roots of my father's humble, thoughtful, and loving nature.

Thomas J. Nordyke, M.D.

The first statement glued in Bob Nordyke's 1932
teen-age scrapbook of important thoughts.

PREFACE

"I'm third": "God is first, everyone else is second, and I'm third."

Friends, family, patients, and professional colleagues of Robert A. Nordyke always recognized his outstanding qualities, caring perceptions, and thoughtful vision. But how did he develop these characteristics? What were the significant influences that molded this remarkable man?

A glimpse of his life through Depression years may help to identify some of the persons, events, and philosophical encounters that shaped his thinking and contributed to his admired pattern of life. In an old box of his mementoes tucked away high on a closet shelf, a scrapbook was uncovered that included meaningful statements carefully preserved by Bob Nordyke during his impressionable teen-age years. The first entry, placed in the center of a large empty page, was "I'm Third".

My father, Ralph G. Cole, an early twentieth century YMCA executive, often told the inspirational story of "I'm third" at YMCA campfire programs. He lived by the principles of those words, as did my husband, Bob Nordyke. This story explains the meaning of "I'm third":

A boy named Jerry spent four very popular years in high school, where he won honors in scholarship, athletics, student government, and many other activities. When he went away to college, his first act upon entering his room was to place above his bed a crude sign in his own handwriting. It said: "I'm third".

The boys who came into his room were curious and asked the meaning of this strange sign. Jerry, however, would not tell even his closest friends, except to say: "I'll explain it on the day I graduate."

During his college years, Jerry was elected president of the student council and captain of the football team, played center on the basketball team, and was chosen the most popular man in school. He was everyone's friend, and he always went out of his way to be helpful and kind. Still, he would not explain the meaning of the "I'm third" sign above his bed.

On the morning of his graduation, a group of boys came to his room to remind him of his promise to tell the significance of the sign that had hung on the wall for four years. "Well," Jerry reluctantly responded, "before I came to college, my mother said, 'Always remember, son, no matter what your successes or failures, God comes first, everyone else comes second, and you are third. Whatever happens, your life will be happy and successful if you remember that motto and live accordingly.' The reason that I didn't want to explain the meaning of the sign was because I was afraid I couldn't make good."

There was a long pause. It was an eloquent silence, a wonderful tribute to Jerry's life in school. It was like a moment of prayer, for every person who had looked into his eyes had known a friend. Now they understood why he had not asked for things for himself, why his friends were glad to trust him and thrust honors upon him.

A classmate spoke up: "Now we understand; you have made good on that motto, and everyone here knows it!"

Bob Nordyke's life exemplifies the pattern of a person who followed the precepts of "I'm third." A gentle, unassuming, gracious, kind, intelligent, humble, generous, and thoughtful family man, he was a deep thinker, a lover of poetry and literature, a pioneer in nuclear medicine, a nationally and internationally recognized teacher, an innovator in medical practice, a clinician, and a researcher.

Always restrained in his actions, he allowed others to go ahead of him ("everyone else is second"): at his medical clinic, he graciously accepted a basement office (considered a less desirable location by many of his colleagues); he encouraged co-workers to share authorship of his scientific writings; when driving the car, he politely slowed to enable others to turn left in front of him; in games, he often helped a losing player to win. His warm personality showed no prejudice or intolerance, and his peacemaking charm and wit dispelled hostility and promoted friendship. Each person who knew him—family member, friend, patient, or professional colleague—felt his rare humanism as they received his total attention. His high standard of excellence reflected an inspiring character with enduring influence.

In the newspaper article "Nordyke was one of our treasures" that appeared after his death on August 23, 1997, George Chaplin, former editor of *The Honolulu Advertiser*, wrote:

> Voltaire said: 'Men who are occupied in the restoration of health to other men, by the joint exertion of skill and humanity, are above all the great of the earth. They even partake of divinity, since to preserve and renew is almost as noble as to create.'
>
> Many of Hawaii's physicians merit such an encomium, but none more than the late Dr. Robert A. Nordyke. He is well recognized as a pioneer in nuclear medicine, but how many know his background, his formative years that made him into the multi-faceted person that he was? [See Appendix, p. 157.]

In 1992 Bob was urged by family and friends to write about his own experiences as a boy growing up in the small California town of Woodland in Sacramento Valley during the post World War I period and the depression years, extending from 1919 to 1950. Over the next five years he sat at his computer and recorded some short episodes in his life that he had used as bedtime stories for his children and grandchildren. This book is a compilation of those adventures. It is not intended as a diary that reports day-to-day and month-to-month activities; instead, it offers scenes of true-life experiences of an American boy growing up in an historical period of the first half of the twentieth century.

If asked why he preserved these family stories, Bob Nordyke might have quoted author Czeslaw Milosz:

> If I mention my ancestors, it is because they are a source of strength for me. Thanks to them, the clothing and the furniture of past epochs, the handwriting on yellowed documents, are not completely dead objects. The awareness of one's origins is like an anchor line plunged into the deep, keeping one within a certain range. Without it, historical intuition is virtually impossible . . . [Milosz, Czeslaw, *Native Realm*, 1968:20]

At the time of his final illness, Bob helped to assemble the chapters for this book, and a preliminary copy was submitted for copyright. Unfortunately, after his death, outlines for additional chapters were found in his desk drawer. While these memoirs may be incomplete, enough information exists in his writings to offer a personal glimpse of the rare human nature and development of this remarkable person.

Many friends and relatives assisted in the preparation of this book. Floyd E. Brown and wife, Carol Edgecomb Brown, shared the memoirs of Floyd's mother, Maurine Brown, who offered fascinating descriptions of her pioneer life in California. Bob Nordyke was intrigued and inspired by her writings.

In 1992 Ralph and Susan Cole accompanied us on a return visit to Pike City. Bob vividly recalled the warmth of family life despite simplicities and limitations of residing in a remote Sierra mountain village, where the family occupied an unheated wooden house and his mother taught eight grades in a single-room country school during the Depression years of 1932–33. He looked upon the experience as "one of the best years of my life!"

Other persons contributing to this project include Aimee M. Grace, eldest granddaughter and a steady companion, who sat on her grandfather's lap to listen to the bedtime tales, memorized his favorite poems, and assisted in the preparation of the manuscript for this book. All of his children—Mary Ellen Nordyke-Grace, Carolyn N. Cozzette, Thomas J. Nordyke, Susan (Nunu) N. Bell, and Gretchen (Nini) N. Worthington; their spouses—Robert A. Grace, J. Michael Cozzette, Michelle Nordyke, Douglas T. Bell, and DuWayne Worthington; and the grandchildren—the Grace children (Aimee, Nalani, Cameron, Trevor, and Noelle), the Cozzette children (Andy and Jennifer), the Nordyke children (Larissa, Nica, and Jay), the Worthington children (Kaylin and Mark), and the soon to be born Bell child—eagerly encouraged the publication of a written form of their grandfather's familiar true life stories.

Many relatives helped to locate illustrations for some of the stories. Bob's siblings—Betty Nordyke Scher with daughter Linda Scher Padilla, James P. Nordyke with daughter Carol Nordyke Gentry, Helen Nordyke Krug with daughter Nancy R. Kubik—searched photo albums and boxes. Thanks are expressed to Milan Heger who offered cartoon drawings, adding: "I will always remember my American hero Dr. Bob Nordyke, the best man I've ever known."

Appreciation for cooperation on this project is extended to Twyla R. Thompson of the Chamber of Commerce of Woodland and to Ron Pinegar and Susan Bovey of the City of Woodland Historical Preservation Committee. Rene Buchmüller, Max Millard, and Thomas Fleming generously shared their photos.

We especially want to thank the staff of Barbara Pope Book Design, including Barbara Pope, Maureen Liu-Brower, Tia Reber, and Elizabeth Lee, for their enthusiastic support and kind, careful, and thorough shepherding of the manuscript and illustrations through the publication process.

We are grateful to special friends—Don Anderson, Bill and Connie Burlingame, George Chaplin, Robert R. and Esther Dye, Dr. Norman and Ramsay Goldstein, E. Chipman Higgins, Mary S. Judd, Tomoki Kanaoka, Kent Keith, Chris and Casimir Kulikowski, Richard R. Lowe, Paula and William Merwin, Sylvia Mitchell, Yoneko Narita, Shirley M. Nordyke, Dr. Sada Okumura, Ellen Pyle, Hilma and William E. Wire, Kenneth Worthington, and many others—who reviewed some chapters and contributed information, assistance, maps, and pictures to make this work possible.

Eleanor C. Nordyke

Graduation from the
University of California San Francisco
School of Medicine at Berkeley, California in 1951.

If hind'rances obstruct thy way,
Thy magnanimity display,
     And let thy strength be seen.
But O! If fortune fill thy sail
With more than a propitious gale,
     Take half thy canvas in.

HORACE
[QUINTAS HORATIUS FLACCUS]
BOOK II, ODE X

Bob holds brother Jim on his lap, while sisters
Betty and Helen and a pet goat stand nearby in 1925.

Chapter One

೪೪ EARLY DAYS ೪೪

I was born on July 14, 1919, in Woodland, California. All I know about that event is contained in a scrapbook my mother kept. On the birth certificate my first name was handwritten in beautiful script as "Byron," to honor my dad for his good work in producing me.

By some act of God that nobody has yet explained and for which I have been forever grateful, the name was changed to "Robert." My middle name was "Allan," right from the beginning. It was the last name of a fellow student of my mother's at Columbia University who later became president of Bennington College in Vermont. The French have celebrated my birthday ever since, calling it "Bastille Day."

The Town

Woodland is a little town that nestles amidst the lush, flat farmlands of the Sacramento Valley between the Coast Range and the Sierra Nevada mountains. Sacramento, the capital of California, lies twenty miles to the east, on the far side of the Sacramento River which collects the mountain streams and provides water to nourish the whole valley. Davis, six miles to the south, is now the home of a major campus of the University of California, but in the 1920's and 1930's it was an agricultural college. Each year my dad would take me there to visit the State Agricultural Fair. We'd stand on the curb, ice cream cones dripping, as the parade passed by, involve ourselves in the livestock competition (Dad often served as one of the judges) and excitedly watch prancing five-gaited horses and harness races from the stands.

Woodland had a population of about 5,000 people. Its economic base was farming. Main Street ran through its center where nearly all of the businesses were lined up, including my dad's butcher shop near Second Street. All streets crossed Main exactly at right angles, in an orderly fashion, like tick-tack-toe. They were given predictable names such as First, Second, and Third Streets. Beyond First they became less predictable, like College, which led to the high school.

The tracks of the Sacramento Northern Railway, an electric train that transported business people and students back and forth to Sacramento, ran down the middle of Main Street, curving into a covered station on Second. My sister Virginia boarded the train each Monday morning to attend Sacramento Junior College, and returned home on it

Grandmother Nordyke

Byron A. Nordyke,
father

Grandfather Nordyke

Merle B. Nordyke with Betty and infant Bob.

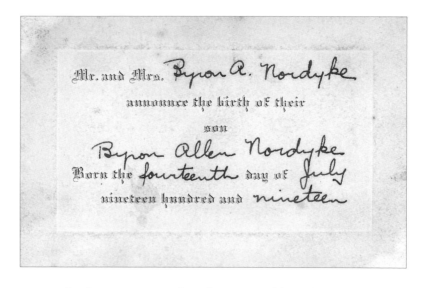

Birth announcement for Robert A. Nordyke, July 14, 1919.

Grandfather and Grandmother Nordyke's home was in Berkeley, California, southwest of the little town of Woodland where Bob was born.

Woodland, a small town in Northern California, is located between the Coast Range and the Sierra Nevada mountains.

OPPOSITE

The historic area of the city of Woodland, California, is situated between Main and Pendegast Streets and Elm and Third Streets.

Woodland, California - 1925

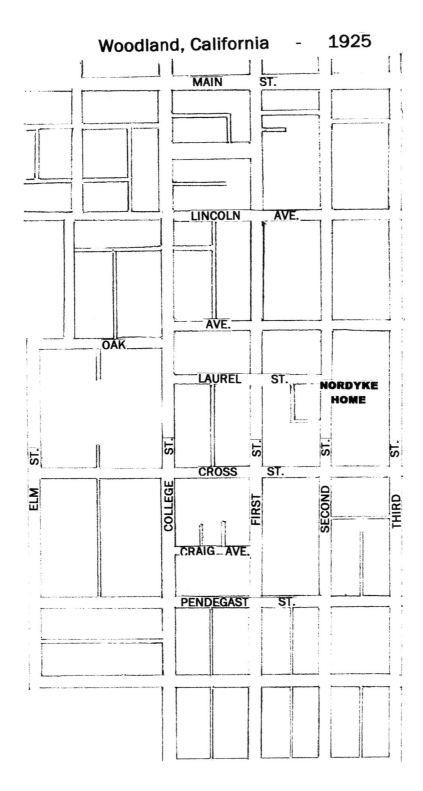

"All streets crossed Main exactly at right angles, in an orderly fashion, like tick-tack-toe."

The Sacramento Northern Railway ran down the middle of Main Street

each Friday night. In town it drew its electric power from overhead lines, but once out of town it was powered from a "third rail."

No commercial building I can remember stood as high as three stories except for the imposing Bank of Italy, which dominated Main Street. During the early 1900's the people were proud to have an "opera house" that was used for town meetings, plays, and an occasional light opera from San Francisco. By the time I was born, boards were nailed over its door, and signs and cobwebs indicated that it was closed.

The town was compact. Woodland High School and Beamer Elementary School, at opposite sides of town, were within walking distance for most students. Beautiful shade trees lined both sides of the streets—elms, black walnuts, palms—to provide at least some escape from the 112+ degree summer sun, and some beauty too. The cement sidewalks were wide enough for rollerskating, playing hop-scotch, and bicycle riding when your mother wanted you to stay off the streets.

Most of the homes resembled typical modest mid-American residences. Nearly every house had a well kept lawn in front and porches that were sometimes screened off to keep out gnats and flies in the summertime. On hot nights older people sat on the porches in rocking chairs, fanning themselves, visiting with friends. Scattered here and there were large, white, three-story, corner houses with high, round, embossed turrets, reminding me of old castles. Windows looked out from them in all directions. These homes were often encircled by wide lawns and shaded by huge oak trees. Soft red and yellow leaves floated down from them in the fall.

"Scattered here and there were large, white, three-story, corner houses with high, round, embossed turrets, reminding me of old castles." Homes of neighbors (clockwise from upper left): Edward I. Leake, newspaper editor; John Hart, Yolo county farmer; Edmund R. Lowe, businessman; Dr. Fred Fairchild, family physician.

The Weather

The weather in Woodland and the surrounding Sacramento Valley left something to be desired, but we kids didn't recognize that at the time. It was just the way weather came. Summer was sweltering. Sometimes it got so hot by mid-July that when we walked across Main Street our bare feet would sink half an inch into the tar. We'd have to race to the other side, sit on a curb, and fan our feet. When the strong, gusty north winds swept across the Valley, walnuts would drop down onto the yards and streets and collect in the gutters. We'd rake them into gunnysacks and sell them for fifty cents a sack.

In winter it was often cold and rainy. Sometimes rainwater poured down the street gutters, widening out at driveways and slurping down grated manholes. The rushing torrents made wonderful rivers for sailing boats that we carved out of pieces of wood with our pocketknives. When leaves and sticks blocked the outlets, a whole street corner would fill with water. That was even better. The sidewalks became slick and smooth in the rain, so when we raced our bicycles we could slam on the brakes and spin around in full circles without falling off.

The Neighborhood

Our home was three blocks south of Main, past the Episcopal Church, at 637 Second Street. It was a good neighborhood, I thought. On one side was an older, very proper couple, Mr. and Mrs. Hart. Both were round faced and a bit plump. Mr. Hart had a trim, white mustache, and the top of his head was bald. They seemed old, maybe in their fifties or sixties, and they often sat on their screened wooden porch. You could hear the rhythmic squeak of their rocking chairs in the evenings. Their house and yard were immaculately groomed. The front lawn was terraced, and the grass was kept green and short. In the backyard they grew a vegetable garden and maintained an aviary. It held thirty or forty pigeons that flew out of the open door and around town every day, fluttering back into the aviary in the evening.

We couldn't have been the best neighbors for them. They were childless, while seven children lived in our home. Often we kids swung from our tree house in the branches of a grafted English walnut tree, landing on their manicured hedge. Sometimes, when it took too long to walk around, we broke our way through the hedge to find a ball we hit into their backyard. Despite all that, and to our continual surprise, every Easter the Harts invited our whole family over to hunt eggs that they had hidden for us. When we moved away I heard they became melancholy. Both died shortly after that.

On the opposite side of our house, over our fence, an alley led to the Woodland Clinic & Hospital where I was born. Across the alley was a home for nursing students. When I was a teenager I'd sometimes shut the lights off in our upstairs bathroom at night and try to see something exciting through their windows.

Directly across the street Ed Leake, the publisher of the Woodland Daily Democrat, lived with his wife and son Paul. Paul often tried, unsuccessfully, to date my sister Virginia, who somehow didn't take to him. Anyway, she had lots of other boyfriends.

My most indelible memory of Mr. Leake was when our saddle horse, George, escaped from our backyard one early morning, trotted across the street to his newly-planted front lawn, and casually munched on the sprouting green grass before dropping fertilizer on it and proceeding up the road to our ranch. The hoof-prints sank down about six inches with each step, and there were lots of steps. The fault was laid on me; I hadn't locked the gate. I was given the job of raking and replanting the lawn. Later Mr. Leake became head of the California Board of Equalization in San Francisco. He wrote a letter to our family telling us what he remembered about our father, and what a fine man he was.

The Nordyke children in 1928.
Clockwise from top: Jim, Bob, Helen, and Betty.

Two maiden ladies lived next to Mr. Leake. My only contact with them was when a big dog climbed on top of my little girl dog. I didn't like that, so I hit him on the back with a stick. One of the ladies called loudly from her porch and told me not to do that. She said it was "nature."

The House

Our house itself fit in well with the neighborhood. It was white and two-storied, with a basement underneath. Five steps led up to the porch and main entrance. In front was a lawn covered with tough Bermuda grass bisected by a cement sidewalk. On each side, in the middle of the grass, was a short palm tree with fronds that we could strip off and carve into bows when we played Indian.

I had the duty of cutting the lawn every two weeks in summertime with a lawnmower that I tried to keep sharp with a file. My dad wouldn't let me go to the Tom Mix cowboy Saturday matinee until the lawn was cut and raked with a heavy iron rake that kept getting caught in Bermuda clumps.

One day a man came walking by when I was pushing the lawnmower, puffing and sweating. He stopped to talk, and told me a story.

"Looks like you're doing a good job!" he said. "When I was a young man I was cutting

The family home at 637 Second Street, Woodland, California, 1914 (above).
A return to the family homestead, 1996 (below).

our lawn, just like you. A man came by, stopped, and said to me, 'When I was a young man I was cutting our lawn, just like you. A man came by, stopped, and said to me, "Looks like you're doing a good job!"'"

Then he walked on. I never quite understood that, but I still remember it. It gave me a kind of echoey feeling that we were forever attached to the past.

A graveled driveway led into the backyard to a double garage with sliding doors. Behind the garage was a wonderful hideout. Brother Jim almost burned the garage down when he was playing with matches there. The backyard itself seemed huge—big enough for us to dig trenches that fanned out in all directions. We covered them with boards and shoveled dirt on top to make secret, dark tunnels.

Over on the Harts' side was our tree house, built hodgepodge in the spreading branches of the huge English walnut tree that Dad had grafted onto a sturdy black walnut stump. It was close enough to our back porch roof so we could climb out the second story window onto the roof and jump across to the tree house in our pajamas to sleep there all night.

The basement could be entered through a low window on the driveway side where men shoveled coal in winter and I had to re-shovel it into proper piles inside, or by the main stairs that went down from inside the back porch. It was dark down there, even with the small incandescent electric lights on. At the bottom of the stairs and over in the corner at eye level were wonderfully arranged circles of spider webs attached together like spokes on a wheel. In the middle were intensely black, round spiders with bright red hourglass figures underneath. Their eight legs attached to the vibrating web like they were waiting for something to pass by. Dad said they were "black widows" and we shouldn't get near them. Their bite can be dangerous.

Inside the front door a large hallway led into the main living room where we spent most of our time on wintry days. A cold and uninviting front room was kept neat and tidy for guests. From the hallway a stairway curved upward, leading to the second floor bedrooms. A smooth oak banister was intended to keep us from falling over. In the morning, coming down to breakfast, we could sit on it, one leg on each side, and slide all the way down, sailing around the curve and dropping off at the bottom. Mother didn't like us to do that.

Once I dropped a cloth-covered rock from the top of the stairs on my sister Betty who was standing in the hallway below. It hit her on the head and made her cry. I was sorry about that. I only meant to attract her attention.

An elk-head hung onto the wall at the bottom of the stairs. Its spreading horns acted as a hat rack. Sometimes we'd spin our hats from a distance to see if they'd hook on, like horseshoes. I think it was a trophy from Dad's earlier hunting days.

The mantel above the living room fireplace held a wonderful old brass clock in the center that had all kinds of embellishments around its sides including a statue of the Roman

"A wonderful old brass clock that had all kinds of embellishments,
including a statue of the Roman god Mercury."

god Mercury. Its numbers were written in Roman numerals, and every quarter hour it chimed out the time, like Big Ben. It had to be wound up each Sunday with a metal key that was put into a hole in its face and turned with clicking sounds until it was tight. Over the years that clock gathered a life of its own, a treasure representing our childhood. Each of us children wanted it. When our family moved away from Woodland, sister Helen somehow took it with her. She promised Jim that she'd pass it on to him.

Much of the time my job included stoking the fireplace. When we had money (when Dad was a butcher, rancher, and mayor of the town—before the Great Depression), I brought up kindling and coal from the basement. Later, when coal was too expensive, Dad and I went out to the railroad tracks and picked up old railway ties. They were about six feet long and eight inches thick. In the backyard I set the ties across two sawhorses and cut them with a big cross-cut saw. That wasn't easy because the ties were filled with little rocks embedded into them by passing trains. The grating sound was like scratching your fingernails on a chalkboard.

On wintry days, when it was too cold to play outside, we kids would lie on the floor in front of the fire and avidly read from the Book of Knowledge. The blue, leather-covered set had fascinating sections on poetry, short stories, history, and geography. The pages titled "Things to Make and Things to Do" gave us new ideas, like how to build a house with match sticks.

*"On wintry days, when it was too cold to play outside, we kids would lie on the floor
in front of the fire and avidly read from The Book of Knowledge."*

Mother and Dad's bedroom, with its attached bathroom, was directly off the living room. One day when I was about six, my sister Mary Lou's boy friend (later her husband), Robert Hardison, came to visit her from Stanford University in an old model-T Ford he had borrowed. They were sitting on the couch in the living room, talking. From the bedroom I looked through the keyhole and watched them. Then I wrote a note on a piece of paper and slipped it under the door. It said, "I see you."

In the center of the dining room was a big oak table, rounded at the end. Leaves could be added or taken away, depending on how many guests we had. The chairs were heavy and square; they made you sit up straight, like you're supposed to anyway. "Dinner" was at six in the evening except on Sundays when it was at noon, after church. Meat and potatoes with lots of butter and gravy were the usual fare since that's what Dad liked and we had plenty of meat from our shop.

I didn't like spinach. One day Mother told me I couldn't leave the table until I finished my spinach, so, when no one was looking, I stuffed what was left of the juicy spinach into the front pockets of my jeans and went out to play. It worked fine except that I got busy and forgot about it. Later when Mother washed my clothes she found dried spinach in my pockets.

Back of the dining room was the kitchen. What I remember best about that were two things: washing dishes and eating chocolate. We kids alternated clearing the table, sweeping the floor, washing the dishes, drying the dishes, and putting them away. There were occasional squabbles about whose turn it was to do what, but in general it worked pretty well since we had so many kids.

Chocolate was another thing. High up on the second shelf Mother always kept a tall can of Ghirardelli's sweet ground chocolate—too high for little boys to reach. But I found a way to get up on a chair, stand on the counter, reach up high, and carefully pull down the big, round, yellow can, being sure nobody was looking. Inside the can was a measuring spoon, convenient for taking a taste—only it never was just a taste. One after another spoonful was devoured, sending the powder into my nose and face. Nobody ever caught me at this occupation, but I still sneeze every time I eat chocolate. Some believe it's because of an allergy developed at the time, others that it's from a leftover guilt for taking something without asking.

The back porch was screened in, overlooking the yard. I can still hear the squeaky sound of the screen door that led outside as it banged itself shut by a taut spring. Often Dad hung big bunches of green bananas from a hook on the porch ceiling, waiting for them to ripen to a brilliant yellow. Once I had unaccountable stomach pains that came on after I ate seven green ones.

The porch was the center of ice cream production, too. The makings were put into a shiny gallon steel container that was surrounded by ice with rock salt added. Each of us kids turned the handle until the ice cream became too stiff to move. Dad always had the first taste. My brother Jim and I still have this terrible craving for ice cream. The feeling probably was born there on the porch.

The Runaway

I didn't like Grandmother Binkley, Mother's strict and proper mother. She didn't let me do what I wanted. Her face was soft and crinkly when she kissed me. There were always strained feelings between her and my dad, and he seemed to act differently when she was near. Dad was never quite good enough for her daughter. Besides that, Grandmother whispered to me, he was a drinker. She told me he stopped to get a beer at the saloon before coming home. Had to, I guess, to face her. She saved little bits of string and rolled them up in a ball; they might be useful some time. She thought it was immoral to play cards or dance on Sunday.

Some of her stories about when she was a young teacher near Hollister were interesting, though. Once she taught a class of teen-age students and half of them were Mexican. One day none of the Mexican children came to school. When they returned next day she asked them why. "Maria and Jose got married. We all went to watch them make a baby!"

Grandmother Binkley (right) standing with a friend.

I didn't like to stay with Grandmother Binkley alone. One Sunday when I was five years old it was carefully explained to me that my mother and father were going away for a day and I was to stay with Grandmother. I remember sitting on the porch beside her, weakly waving goodbye to my parents as their car drove off, with tears in my eyes.

That did it! I wasn't going to stay with her. I was going to run away from home. Where didn't matter. Anywhere.

When Grandmother Binkley wasn't looking I gathered up my pajamas, toothbrush, and favorite top, put them in a paper bag, and started down the road. At Main Street I turned left, headed out of town, towards the Flyers Club.

Before long I got tired of walking and was about to lie down on the roadside when I saw an airplane above me, flying low overhead, crossing the road. Other planes were taking off and landing in a field close by. Most of them had two cockpits, with the pilots' heads sticking out over the top where you could see them. They wore helmets and goggles, just like in the movies.

I went over to the field, climbed up on a wooden fence, and watched with fascination as the planes landed and took off in front of me. I'd never been so close to moving airplanes before. That's what I'd like to do when I grow up, I thought. Fly high in the sky.

A long time must have passed when I felt something touch my shoulder. Turning around, I saw a big man wearing a uniform, with a flashing star on his dark blue shirt.

Kindergarten class, 1924: Bob sits in the middle of row one.

"Are you Bobby Nordyke?"

"Yes."

"Your mommy and daddy are looking for you!"

"Oh?"

"That's right. Come with me and I'll take you home."

I wasn't sure about that idea. But then again, I hadn't eaten for a long time, and home sounded good.

The Hospital

I've heard that hospitals are good places to stay away from. You can get worse instead of better. On the other hand, if you get hurt and have to get something fixed, they can take good care of you.

I tried to stay away from the Woodland Clinic except for being born there. For one thing, when I passed by on my bicycle it had this kind of sweet smell, like ether. They were probably putting people to sleep so the doctors could operate on them.

But one day I had to go to the hospital myself. I was cranking the Willys-Knight car in our garage to get it started for Dad, who was in the driver's seat. Usually he set the spark so the engine wouldn't kick the crank back in the reverse direction. Well, that day two things went wrong at the same time: Dad didn't set the spark right, and I had my thumb wrapped around the crank handle when I had been told never to do that. It kicked back, and I went howling up into the air, holding on to my arm in pain.

Dad jumped out of the car to see what had happened. There was a deep hollow in the middle of my right arm. It hurt—badly! So right away he took me through the alleyway behind our house to the Clinic, a hundred yards away, and into Dr. Fairchild's office. The doctor twisted it and asked me if it hurt. I said it did and told him not to do that any more.

A nurse put my arm under an x-ray machine. A few minutes later, out came a picture of the bones in my arm. What a sight! He showed me the broken bone on a light box, and said he was going to fix it—now. All I had to do was put my arm on a table between two sand bags, be a good boy and not move. Dr. Fairchild asked the nurse to hold my hand and pull while he took a little round wooden dowel, placed it on the spot that hurt most, and hit it sharply with a hammer.

"Did that hurt?" he asked.

"Not much," I answered, wincing.

He hit the dowel with the hammer again. That hurt. But he let me know he was almost done. One more hit.

"Fine! It's in place now. Let's put it in a cast."

Woodland Clinic and Hospital at Third and Cross Streets.

So the nurse wrapped my arm with long strips of white, soggy, plaster-filled gauze, leaving the fingers out, and let it dry. She gave me a sling and sent me home. Mother was surprised.

My brothers and sisters wrote their names on the cast. In a week it got awfully itchy in the palm of the hand underneath. I scratched, pulling off pieces of skin, leaving red, new skin underneath. It felt better that way.

My dad didn't have enough money to pay the doctor. I went with him when he carried a dressed sheep to the hospital to pay the bill.

One Saturday afternoon a year later I was playing tennis on the elementary school tennis court with two of the Scarlett boys, when I knocked the ball over the fence and into a large pile of palm fronds. Climbing onto the pile, looking for the ball, I slipped, fell, and suddenly had a terrible, sharp pain in the middle of my left leg. The boys pulled me off the pile and looked at the leg. Nothing there! I held on to them and tried to walk. Every step hurt so much I couldn't stand it. I held on to them and tried to hobble. It hurt too much to hobble. So I sat on the ground.

One of them ran to their home across the schoolyard to get his mother (my mother's best friend, Stella), who brought a little red wagon from her house. Together they pulled me across the yard to a car, got me inside, and drove me to the Clinic, hurting with every jiggle.

Oh, oh—Dr. Fairchild again!

"You're having a hard time staying away from here, son," he said. "What did you do to yourself this time?"

Second Grade class, 1926: Bob stands in the middle of row one.

Woodland Elementary School Report

Bobby Nordyke

Grade 2?

Term Commencing Jan 24 1927

	1st Qr.	2nd Qr.	3rd Qr.
TARDINESS	0	0	0
DAYS ABSENT	16	0	14
DEPORTMENT	B	C+	C+
NEATNESS	a	a	a
EFFORT	B	B	B
ATTENTION	a	a	a
ARITHMETIC {Written/Mental}	a	a	a
SPELLING	a	a	a
ENGLISH Composition			
GEOGRAPHY			
HISTORY Civil Government			
HYGIENE			
READING {Memorizing/Literature/Phonics/Home Read.}	a	a	a
WRITING	B	B	a
NATURE STUDY			
DRAWING			
MUSIC			
BOOKKEEPING			
MAN'L TRAINING			
PHYS. TRAINING			

_____ Teacher.

Woodland Elementary School Report

Bobby Nordyke

High/Low — High 3 Grade

Term Commencing Sept. 6 1927

	1st Qr.	2nd Qr.	3rd Qr.	Avg
TARDINESS				
DAYS ABSENT			3	3
DEPORTMENT	a	B	C+	B
NEATNESS	B	a	B	B
EFFORT	a	a	a	
ATTENTION	a	a	a	a
ARITHMETIC {Written/Mental}	a	a	C+	B
	a	a	a	a
SPELLING	a	a	a	
ENGLISH Composition	a	a	a	
GEOGRAPHY				
HISTORY Civil Government				
HYGIENE				
READING {Memorizing/Literature/Phonics/Home Reading}	a	B	a	a
	a	a	a	a
	a	a	a	a
WRITING	C+	B	B	B
NATURE STUDY				
DRAWING	C+	B	B	B
MUSIC				
BOOKKEEPING				
MAN'L TRAINING				
PHYS. TRAINING				

Blanche Grigsby, Teacher.

Report cards, second and third grades.
Bobby's deportment offered a challenge for his elementary school teachers.

"I don't know. It just hurts!"

He examined my leg. Nothing could be seen. Whenever he moved my leg I let out a howl. They took an x-ray. Nothing there! He felt more deeply. Nothing there!

"You must be kidding us!"

Then he put a probe down a little hole next to my shin bone. Maybe something was there. I could hear a scraping sound. He pushed a little harder. It hurt. With long-nosed silver pliers he caught on to an object and pulled it out.

"Gosh! Look at that!" he exclaimed, "You weren't kidding!"

Glistening at the end of his pliers was a long, dark, three inch tapered stick, sharp on one end and broken off on the other. When he held it up to the light for a better look, Dr. Fairchild announced that the dried tip of a palm frond had gone nearly through my leg, not quite out the other side, and had broken off just beneath the skin at the entry point. X-rays don't see wood, only metal, he said. I wished I could be a doctor.

I kept the frond tip on our fireplace mantle next to the clock to show it to my friends. A scar is still there on the front of my leg.

Dad took another sheep to the hospital.

Scarlet Fever

It was summertime, 1929. No school. The Saturday matinees had started, with Hoot Gibson and Buck Jones riding high, saving beautiful girls from certain death as their carriages careened to the cliff's edge ("Don't miss the sequel next Saturday!").

Right in the middle of these exciting times I suddenly got a sore throat, felt hot, and noticed a myriad of tiny red spots covering my body. Mother called for Dr. Blevins, who looked me over and said it was scarlet fever. There was no treatment; it had to run its own course, and it was very contagious. Officials from the County Department of Health came by our house and tacked up a brilliant red sign on the front door—

QUARANTINE!

Big black letters, below a skull and crossbones, warned everybody to stay away, allowing no one to enter the contaminated household for fear of spreading the disease. Mother and I remained inside. Dad and my brothers and sisters were kept outside, staying with friends.

The next three weeks turned out to be one of the best times of my life. For one thing, I had my mother all to myself, a difficult thing to arrange when she had my dad and six other children to consider. During the first few days I turned and tossed in bed, and she brought medicines and drinks and applied ice-filled hot water bottles to bring down the temperature. At the peak of the fever, over 105 degrees, she sat constantly on the side of the bed, cooling my forehead with compresses. I can still hear her quiet, confident voice guiding me through a hazy near-delirium to sleep:

Lay your cold hand across my brow
And I shall sleep, and I shall dream
Of silver pointed willow boughs
Dipping their fingers in a stream.
     Elinor Wylie

As the fever subsided, my mother had time to sit at my bedside and teach me lines of poetry that were central to her point of view and way of life:

If of thy mortal goods thou art bereft
And from thy slender store two loaves alone to thee are left;
Sell one, and with the dole
Buy hyacinths to feed thy soul.
     Muslih-ud-Din Saadi

The World is too much with us; late and soon,
Getting and spending, we lay waste our powers;
Little we see in nature that is ours;
We have given our hearts away, a sordid boon!
     William Wordsworth

Later we sat together on the screened back porch reading wondrous things about geography, strange people in far away places, and animals. From the *Book of Knowledge* we found that the blue whale was the largest animal on earth, growing 92 feet long. In the backyard we measured 92 feet and sketched out the outlines of a whale. It was big!

On Saturday afternoons my sisters Betty and Helen and brother Jim came home from the movie matinees to relay all the exciting things that they had seen. They sat on the roof of the little garage next door beyond our fence and gave rapid-fire explanations—all at the same time and each with his own slightly different version: how the girl didn't really go over the cliff but was saved at the last moment by Hoot Gibson, who pulled her out of the runaway carriage onto his galloping silver-bridled palomino, and veered to safety while the carriage went over the cliff in flames.

The BB Gun

To this day I don't understand why my dad succumbed to my constant urging to give me a BB gun for Christmas. It was fun, all right, but not the most appropriate gift for a nine year old boy. At least that's my opinion now, looking back on it.

But at the time, nothing could have been better. What a beauty it was! A glistening stock kept bright by neat's-foot oil that caused the slightest scratch to disappear; a lever

*"To this day I don't understand why my dad succumbed to my constant
urging to give me a BB gun for Christmas. It was fun, all right, but not the most
appropriate gift for a 9-year-old boy." Photograph courtesy of Kenneth Worthington.*

cocking mechanism that rolled the next of 15 little round lead BBs into place; a smooth,
shiny metal barrel under-slung with wood that matched the stock; and a variable sight
that let you aim straight and hit the bull's eye at twenty or thirty feet, as you chose.

On Christmas day I raced outside to play with it, heeding my mother's warning to be
careful.

"Don't aim it at anybody. It could put an eye out!"

"I won't. I'll be careful."

My parents' bedroom was on the ground floor, and someone was moving around inside. I decided to take my first shot at the screen over the window, just to rattle it and get
their attention.

Bang! Tinkle tinkle! The BB went right through the screen, made a little hole in the
center of the window, and splintered the glass out to its edges like the spokes of a wheel.
How embarrassing!

Responding to my dad's angry tones, I said, "I'm sorry. I didn't think it would go
through the screen. I'll never do it again."

He and I worked all afternoon putting in new glass.

Across the street behind Mr. Leake's house an alleyway provided entry to garages and
backyards between the First and Second Street houses. Now that I owned a BB gun, one
garage was particularly enticing. It belonged to the Worcesters. Their daughter had been
my first grade teacher. On the alley side, two large windows decorated most of the garage
wall, each made up of maybe a dozen small panes, three or four inches square. Many of
them were broken, but a few remained intact. All were covered with cobwebs. It wasn't
like it would hurt anything if you shot out the ones that were left.

So I found an old broomstick, put it between my legs, and galloped back and forth
past the garage windows, firing on the run, holding the gun in one hand and the horse in
the other, like they showed in the matinees. With each passing shot I was getting better

and better at knocking out the remaining unbroken glass that splattered to the ground beneath.

That went on for ten or fifteen minutes. Then, suddenly, I felt the presence of a dark figure standing in the garage shadows, quietly watching. It was Mr. Worcester. I pulled my "horse" to a stop, and sheepishly said hello.

"What are you doing to my windows, Bobby?"

"I've been practicing with my new BB gun. Most of the panes were already broken. I didn't think it would hurt anything."

"I want you to fix them all like new."

"All?"

"All! I'm going to call your daddy right now."

Dad and I spent the better part of two days fixing Mr. Worcester's windows. My allowance for the next two months went to pay for the glass.

Ellwood Williams was one of my best friends. He was a little older, but the gang of us played touch football together and roller skated on the smooth pink sidewalk in front of the Elks Club, practicing all kinds of turns, jumps, and backward team speed skating.

One afternoon after school I took my BB gun and went out hunting for whatever was available. Climbing up onto the roof of a little shed behind Ellwood's house and peering cautiously over the brow of the roof, I spied something extraordinary. Mrs. Williams, plump and well padded, was leaning over, picking petunias.

What a terrible dilemma! What should I do? The BB wouldn't hurt her. On the other hand, it wouldn't be very nice. But then, what an opportunity!

I aimed, fired, heard a little yelp, slipped backwards down the roof, jumped off, and ran home. On arrival, Mother already had the story.

The BB gun was taken away permanently.

Jim
Scarlett.

?
?

Betty
Nordyke

Merle Nordyke.
Jim Nordyke
& Dan Scarlett

Pat
Scarlett

Stella
Scarlett.

Bob
Nordyke.

?
?

Helen
Nordyke.

Lee
Scarlett

A picnic with family and friends near Woodland in northern California in 1928.
Bob (center front) holds spring wildflowers.

Chapter Two

∾ CHILDHOOD IMPRESSIONS ∾

The Country

A short distance out of the little town of Woodland the country flowed in all directions, as far as you could see. It was within walking distance, too. In the summertime fields of alfalfa, wheat, grapes, and melons filled the air with pungent smells. The heavy scent of freshly mown hay still brings back memories. On the corner of each section (640 acres) a large, white, gabled house usually marked the home of a prosperous farmer and his family.

To get to my dad's ranch I'd hike north to the end of Third Street, skip along a paved road a few hundred yards, and cross the railroad tracks past a sign made like a big X with black letters that read: "Private property, permission to pass over revocable at any time" (I didn't understand what that meant). Then I'd turn down our lane, a narrow graveled road a quarter of a mile long with a high center and low sides deepened by truck wheels and horses' hooves. Barbed wire fences lined both sides of the road.

Beyond the fence on the left side ran the glistening railroad track that converged off into the distance, accented by crossties blackened by creosote. Some days, when there was plenty of time in the sultry summer days, I would lean against the fence, chew on a dry grass stem, watch the smoke from an oncoming engine fold back over rumbling freight cars, and wave to the engineer. It pleased me when he tipped his striped hat and smiled back as he pulled a cord to blow the steam whistle, slacken the train's momentum, and watchfully proceed towards the depot. At the end of our lane alternating red lights and clanging bells stopped traffic while he passed by. Some days I could count as many as fifty freight cars—empty flat ones, oil tankers, and two-deckers with crowded sheep peering out between the slats, lying on top of each other, bleating in discomfort. At the very end was the caboose. My dad promised that some day he'd take me to Chicago in a caboose, over the mountains, through the tunnels, onto the plains, and visit the largest stockyards in the world. It might take a week.

On the right side of the lane row on row of stubby grapevines were bent down by long, slim, tightly crowded bunches of Thompson seedless grapes. One of my favorite pastimes was to leap over the barbed wire fence by holding on to a post with both hands, place a tentative foot on the wobbly wire, and swing across, plunking down on the soft dirt of the vineyard. Then I'd choose a vine, lie on my back in its shade, and settle my head

The lush flat farmland of Sacramento Valley. Photograph by Ted Streshinsky.

comfortably on an upturned clod directly beneath a full cluster of white grapes. Leisurely I'd pluck them one by one, brush the dust off on my shirt, and savor each moist, fresh, round, sweet fruit. I'm not sure the farmer would have wanted to share with me, but he never knew I was there.

The Slaughter House

At the end of the lane loomed a hodge-podge group of red buildings. The centerpiece was the two-storied slaughter house. An outside ramp behind it led from a ground-level corral to the second floor. Steers were driven single file up the ramp into a closed chute where they were struck on the head with the blunt end of an axe or shot in the brain with a 30/30 rifle. Then the floor beneath them was tripped open and they slid out into a high-ceilinged room. Here men with bloody hands and aprons slit the throats of the unfortunate steers, positioned a hook beneath their jaws, pushed a button on the wall to start a pulley motor that raised them into hanging position, sliced open their bellies to let the insides out, and yanked off their hides. After that the splattered men turned on a hose, washed off the denuded steers, the floor, and themselves, and pushed the carcasses along the ceiling track that led into the walk-in freezer.

Our Poland China pigs weren't handled any more gently. They were "stuck," bled out, and dropped into a vat of boiling water until their stiff hair softened. Then the men scraped them down to the white skin with a round, cup-like instrument and slid them to the big room and into the freezer. I can still hear the grating sound, like scraping your fingernails on a blackboard.

At the back of the building was a huge pile of rice hulls, maybe 30 feet deep. I don't know why Dad had them put there, but they were too much for us kids to leave alone. We climbed to a second-story window above the pile and dived down onto it, bouncing a little, settling down in its soft comfort, and sliding headfirst down its sides. To our joy, rice hulls scattered everywhere. Mom put a stop to that when I came home, itching. She put me into the bathtub. We counted over a hundred fleas floating about on top of the water and washed them down the drain.

Directly behind the slaughter house towered the red barn. This structure had several purposes—to store alfalfa hay in its loft, feed the horses and beef cattle with hay raked down from above, and stable the horses. A long trough next to the fence was always kept filled with water through a continuously running hose.

On the far side of the barn a gate opened into the thirty-acre field of alfalfa, the ranch's life blood. With the help of irrigation and the hot summer sun, it produced three full crops each season, enough hay to feed the livestock through the winter. Little levees ran parallel across the field. Water gushed out of a pipe a foot wide, pumped from a well by a gasoline engine. It splashed into the main ditch where it was distributed through a se- ries of guillotine gates that let water into one segment of the field at a time.

Most damage to the crops came from gophers that ate the roots of the growing alfalfa shoots. As water flooded a segment, it would filter down holes and force the gophers up. My job was to stand on a levee and whack them with the back side of a shovel when they came running out. I didn't like that, but it was part of what a farmer's son was expected to do.

As each crop matured, the mowers came out and cut the alfalfa close to the ground, leaving a couple of inches of stubble. Then the horse-drawn rakes gathered the hay into little piles so they'd get completely dry—really dry, my dad emphasized, so when they were forked onto a wagon and hoisted into the barn the moisture wouldn't get hot and cause "spontaneous combustion," whatever that meant.

We couldn't irrigate the far end of the alfalfa field because of a large mound of earth, maybe one hundred yards across and twenty feet high. It wasn't any use to anybody that way, so Dad decided to level it and plant more alfalfa. He hired men with a scraper on front of a Caterpillar tractor to do the job. As the earth unfurled in front of the blade, trinkets of all kinds spilled out, and colored beads and arrowheads. It quickly became ev- ident they were uncovering an Indian burial ground. I was galloping bareback around the field on my pinto pony, watching, fascinated, when one of the men, laughing, tossed up to me a long string of beads—bright, with alternating rings of red and yellow and black. Catching it on the run, I looped it around my neck. But it didn't feel like a string of beads. It was soft and it wiggled. I was startled. So was the little king snake. It wanted off. I agreed. I flipped it from my neck onto the ground where it slithered away, back into the burial ground.

Dad stopped the work and notified a professor at the University of California in Berkeley who knew about Indians. I was glad. Things like that should be saved.

Horses

I've loved horses from the very beginning. There were always several around the ranch. Two I loved especially—Bird and George. My first memory of a horse was Bird. She was already old when I first knew her, and was just right for children. She must have been pure black when she was young, but now the black was mixed with gray. Her back swayed deeply. Once you were lifted up onto her it was hard to fall off. Three or four kids could fit on her back at the same time, all squished together. Rarely did we put a saddle on her; it didn't fit well and didn't do any good, anyway. Her bridle bit was made of two smooth pieces of steel separated in the middle by a ring.

Bob rides George, his dad's cowhorse, at the family ranch.

Bird was gentle but intelligent. Dad often brought her to our backyard on weekends. If she wanted to go somewhere, she went. We kids didn't have too much control from up on top, and sometimes, after a lot of urging and kicking, someone would have to get off and lead her to get her started, then jump back on from a bench we kept for that purpose. We crawled underneath her to show our friends how brave we were.

George was different. He was Dad's favorite cowhorse—a trim sorrel with a white face, white rear leg stockings, a gently curving back, and a long brown mane that floated up and down when he galloped. His bit had a rotating corrugated ring in the middle that let him know instantly which way you wanted him to turn. Walking behind cattle, you could feel his quivering alertness. If one steer bolted from the group, he was off after it instantly, wheeling around on his hind legs, off at full speed in one leap, guiding the errant one back into its proper place. No monkey business. No need for guidance from me. From a fast gallop he could come to a sliding stop and be off in the opposite direction before you could say Jack Robinson. All I had to do was hold on.

I tell you about Bird and George because of a special experience of mine when I was five years old. For reasons I can't remember, I wanted to ride a horse. It was Saturday morning on a hot summer day. I hiked up Second Street to Main, crossed over to Third, went to its end out in the country, turned across the Southern Pacific railroad tracks, and whistled my way down the lane to our ranch. There, to my joy, were Bird and George, saddled and bridled, tied with ropes to a fence, ready for me to ride. Wow!

I chose Bird—easier to handle. Climbing up on the fence to mount her (I was too small to reach the stirrups), she moved her rear end away from the fence, at right angles, so I couldn't get on. Down I climbed, and pushed her back against the fence. She was compliant, but when I climbed up the fence again she repeated her performance, moving her rear end straight out.

Enough of that! I'll ride George. He minded better. He didn't move when I climbed the fence and got on. Untying the rope, worming my feet between the leather straps above the stirrups, cross-neck reining to let him know which way to go (Dad had taught me that by making me turn round and round a big oak tree in the middle of the alfalfa field), and kicking him in the sides to get him started, I was off for a ride. Where? It was about lunchtime. I was getting hungry. Let's go home.

So we went along the lane, turned down Third Street and onto Main. As I rode along in the middle of Main Street, George stopped, right on the tracks of the Sacramento Northern Railway. He wouldn't budge. I kicked him. He wouldn't move. I clucked at him the way my dad had taught me. He still didn't move.

Then I heard a startling thing: the shriek of a train whistle. Looking behind I saw an electric train bearing down on the track where George and I stood, coming up fast. It blew its whistle again. I was too high off the ground to get down from the horse. What shall I do now? George still wouldn't move. The train's wheels squealed, screeching to a stop a few feet away from George and me. Out of the front cab window, high above, a head popped out, and the engineer said something I didn't understand, loudly.

Then a kindly man came up and told me I shouldn't be riding on the street (it was for cars and trains). But he'd help me down. He lifted me off, pulled the reins over George's head, and handed them to me.

"Where do you live?"

"637 Second Street." I had learned that by heart.

"I think you should lead your horse home and tell your daddy."

That sounded like a good idea, so I led George down the sidewalk towards home. It was three blocks away, which gave me time to think. What if Dad didn't like me to ride his horse without asking? What would he do if he found out? Where could I hide the horse? I know! Lock him in the garage, where nobody can find him.

So I turned off the sidewalk into our driveway, George clopping behind, slid open the two-car garage door, pulled him inside and locked him in, bridle hanging loose and saddle still on. Then I went into the house and crawled under a bed.

Mother was on the telephone. I could hear her talking.

"No. I haven't seen your horse. Somebody stole him while you went into town for lunch? Who could have done that? That's terrible!"

I heard Mother telephoning other people to see if they had seen Dad's horse. Nobody had. By this time I was feeling bad, thinking I shouldn't have taken Dad's favorite horse. How can I tell my mother?

I sheepishly crawled out from under the bed and tapped her shoulder while she was on the telephone.

"George is in the garage," I whispered.

"What? I don't believe it!" she said, quickly dropping the telephone receiver onto its hook.

We went outside and I showed her. George's reins were tangled around his legs.

She called my dad, who raced home, fast. He was so happy to find his horse he didn't even scold me.

Five years later, when I was ten, we still had George. He hadn't lost much of his spirit. I was riding him back to the ranch, galloping down our lane towards the barn. Dad and Mom were in their car behind me, planning to pick me up and bring me home after I unsaddled the horse.

George had been out all day. When he turned down the lane toward the barn, it was hard to hold him back. He wanted to go home. He took off in a run. I tried to slow him down by pulling back on the reins as firmly as I could, with little effect.

Half way down the lane I felt the saddle start to slip sideways under me. The cinch had loosened and was flapping under his belly. The saddle slipped farther off George's back, down his side, and finally underneath, bumping his legs. This frightened him, causing him to run even faster.

By then I was riding bareback, racing down the lane, holding onto his neck, unable to pull on the reins, trying to keep from falling off. I was facing down, clinging tightly to his mane. Underneath, gravel was flying in all directions from his pounding hoofs. I was breathing hard, wondering what would happen if I fell off.

Luckily the barn gate was near. George raced right up to it and slid to a jolting stop, throwing me onto his neck. Dad drove up, jumped out of his car, helped me down, and unsaddled George for me. The cinch had come loose, he said.

Mother thought that kind of ride was dangerous. She asked me not to do it again.

Church

We belonged to the Christian Church, not far from our house. My first memory of it was second hand, told to me by my dad. I must have been three years old or so, and was singing a song from the pew, along with everybody else. They finished, but I continued on, loud and clear. Dad tried to hush me up, but others around hushed him up instead, and I went on to finish the song. The audience clapped.

Baptism in the Christian Church was done late, when you were supposed to know what you were doing. The minister dunked you all the way under. My turn came when I was eight years old. Up on the platform near the pulpit they put a small canvas swimming pool that was propped up on four sides. The minister stood outside at the edge, dry, while I wore my bathing suit, standing in the pool in four feet of water. The minister gave me instructions.

"I'll say some things, you hold your breath, and I'll put your head down under water. When you come up, you'll be a Christian."

That sounded OK with me.

I guess I didn't get his instructions right. He started to mumble something that went on and on. I held my breath. Then, when I was almost out of breath, he leaned over, pushed my head under water, and held it there.

I thought he was trying to drown me. I came up fighting, throwing my fists every which way. I hit the minister in the stomach. He let me up. It wasn't what he planned, he said, but he let me be a Christian anyway.

"We belonged to the Christian Church, not far from our house."

One summer I went to Daily Vacation Bible School. At the end of it, the teacher said, she was going to give us all Bibles. If we were really good and attended every day for eight weeks, we'd get a Bible and a paper scroll with our own name printed on it to hang on our wall at home.

I learned a lot that summer, singing songs and memorizing parts of the Bible. The shortest verse in the Bible is "Jesus wept." I could list off the names of all the books in the Old and New Testaments by heart, and even pronounce Deuteronomy. The teacher would start the Twenty Third Psalm, "The Lord is my shepherd . . ." and I could immediately continue, ". . . I shall not want; he maketh me to lie down in green pastures . . ." and say all the rest of it, to the end. When I recited the verses out loud at home, Dad added the one he liked best, "Consider the lilies of the field, how they grow; they toil not, neither do they spin. But Solomon in all his glory was not arrayed like one of these." I learned that one, too.

All went well until the last week of the summer session. The whole family went out into the Coast Range foothills to pick blackberries, and I came home covered with poison oak from head to foot. On Saturday my face was red, puffy, and itchy. My eyes were almost closed, so I could hardly see out. To stop the itching and keep me from scratching and causing scars, Mother covered me with calomine lotion that caked white. In the mirror my face looked like a bloated ghost.

What to do about tomorrow? It was the last day of the Bible School. The teacher would hand out Bibles. If I didn't go, I wouldn't get my scroll. But I looked terrible, and didn't feel good, either. Everyone would laugh at me.

Mother thought I should go anyway. Nobody would mind what I looked like. I thought maybe I should, too. The scroll would hang on my wall forever.

So Mother and I walked to the church, hand in hand, with me dragging a little. To my surprise, when I hesitated at the door of the Sunday School room, everybody looked at me but nobody laughed. I guessed they felt sorry for me. The teacher put me in line, right along with the other children. When it was my turn, she handed me a crisp new Bible with my name inside the front cover.

Then she gave me the scroll. There it was, with my own name printed in broad, black strokes: "Bobby Nordyke. Daily Vacation Bible School, August, 1927."

That made me feel proud. I put it up on my wall next to a framed picture my mother gave me of Sir Galahad standing beside a white horse with the words written underneath, "His strength was as the strength of ten because his heart was pure."

My church was the Christian Church, where I went every Sunday, but over at the Episcopal Church on Second Street Mrs. DuBois, a friend of ours, was the choir director. She was in need of a boy soprano, and she said she would pay me ten cents each Sunday if I'd slip out from my church and run over to sing with her boys choir.

That sounded good to me. It would give enough money—a dime—to go to the movies Saturday afternoons. So each Sunday at quarter to eleven I slipped quietly out of my pew and ran the four blocks to the Episcopal Church, darting in the back door and up to the choir loft. The men and boys were on one side of a wide aisle, with the preacher on our

Bob sang soprano in the boys' choir at St. Luke's
Episcopal Church at 515 Second Street.

right and the huge congregation on our left. The ceiling was very high, and windows were colored bright red and yellow with pictures of Jesus wearing a crown of thorns next to his mother Mary. Across from us, and looking directly at us, were the women and girls. Mrs. DuBois sat in the middle, directing us all from there.

One Sunday I felt some awful rumbling in my stomach, with pains that came on and then subsided, stronger and stronger. I wondered what to do. The Episcopal Church has all kinds of rules about what to do for everything, more than the Christian Church. All I knew was that I had to go to the bathroom, quickly. The preacher was droning on and on. I kept looking across to the opposite loft where Mrs. DuBois was singing away, trying to catch her attention, looking to her for a hint of what to do. I couldn't catch her eye.

Finally I couldn't stand it any more. I walked quickly across in front of the preacher and whispered to Mrs. DuBois:

"I need to go to the bathroom—fast! What shall I do?"

She told me to go up to the altar, genuflect, walk out the side door, turn left, and there I'd find a room that said, "Men."

I ran to the altar, bowed quickly, looked frantically up and down outside but couldn't find the room. Home was down the street three blocks. No choice but to run for it. I raced.

Oh, oh! Too late! Something was running into my pants and down my leg. I hobbled on home, ashamed.

Mother put me in the bathtub and washed my clothes. We didn't tell the others.

Cars

I was four years old when I drove a car for the first time. My dad took me with him to transfer a band of sheep from one pasture to another along a country road. Dad and I were in his Willys-Knight car, moving slowly behind the sheep. Two of his ranch hands were helping, one on each side, hollering and using sticks to keep them in line. A dog raced back and forth behind the sheep, tongue hanging out, nipping at their legs, chasing an errant one that ran off, bringing it back into the fold.

The sheep were in no great hurry, munching grass along the sides, baa-a-ing continuously, and leaving little round black droppings all over the road. Dad put his arm out of the window, pounding on the side of the door and whistling to urge them along.

Then he decided he needed to help the men outside and told me to drive the car. He put it in low gear, moved me over to the driver's side, got out, and stood on the running board. Placing one hand on the steering wheel he directed the car down the road. Then he jumped off, leaving me in charge of the car.

"Me?"

"Go ahead. Drive!"

I'd always wanted to drive my dad's car. So I stood up on the seat, took the wheel firmly in both hands, and steered it slowly up the middle of the road behind the sheep.

What a lot of fun! I banged on the side of the door like Dad did, and tried to whistle (it sounded more like a hiss). The only problem was, I couldn't stop the car. The brake was too far away, and anyhow I didn't know how to use it.

By some good fortune I didn't run over any sheep. Dad jumped in to save the sheep— and me—and I felt very proud that I could drive a car.

Brother Jim learned to drive early, too. He was about four years old when Miss Florence Hershey, a dowager who had been a classmate of my mother's in the Mills College class of '13, came over for tea. She parked her car on the street in front of our house. It was a new green Hudson, with a sloping front end. We kids all gathered around to examine it. What was special about it, Miss Hershey explained, was that you didn't have to crank it to get it started. All you had to do was turn the key and the engine started, just like that! She thought that was especially nice for ladies.

Well, Jim had heard that I once drove a car, so he decided to do the same. He got in to the driver's seat of Miss Hershey's Hudson and turned the steering wheel back and forth until he got tired of doing that. Then he spied the key that was left in the car. He turned it. Lo and behold, it started up and the Hudson moved slowly down the street. It must

The Nordyke family car resembled this 1929 Willys-Knight.

have been in low gear. He stayed in it and kept on steering. The car continued down the street for a block or so. Then somehow it eased into a telephone pole and the engine died.

Miss Hershey kept the car key in her purse after that.

The real driving came later. All of us kids got the knack of it in our big backyard. Dad taught us how to set the spark in the right position before cranking, press the clutch down, put it into low and reverse gears, let the clutch out gently, use the hand and foot throttles, and push down the clutch and brake pedals together if we got too near the fence. Back and forth, back and forth we chugged, from one side of the yard to the other, and sometimes out the driveway nearly to the street. We got pretty good at that.

The day I can't seem to forget was when I was practicing driving and the car was backed up against the fence between our house and the alleyway. Somehow I put it into reverse instead of low gear, stepped on the gas, and broke through the fence backwards. I'm not sure what happened to the car. Dad didn't let me drive it again for a week.

Dr. Charles Noble was our dentist. He and his wife, Gladys, were among our best friends, and our families were very close as we grew up. In 1931 Dr. Noble bought a brand new tan four-door Chrysler. He told me that tan was the best color because it didn't show the dust like black cars did. It was beautiful. Compared to our old Willys-Knight, no smoke came out the exhaust, and its engine purred so softly you could hardly tell it was on. It started just by turning the key.

One day Dr. Noble took some of us to Sacramento. I spent a lot of time telling him what a nice car he had, better than ours. He suddenly pulled over to the side of the highway and asked, "Bob, would you like to drive my car?"

"Would I like to drive it? Wow!"

He moved over, and I went around to the driver's side and climbed in. I took a good look at the steering wheel, the gauges, and the gears. The shifts were the same as in Dad's Willys, so I knew I could handle that. The clutch and brake were the same but they were a little hard to reach. I was tickled pink.

He nodded to me to start up. I put it into low, then shifted to second and to high, and pressed the gas pedal to get it up to speed. How smooth! Before long I glanced at the speedometer. It said 45 miles an hour, then 50, then 55. I looked over to Dr. Noble to see if that was too fast. He didn't seem to mind. He was even chuckling to himself.

With my foot farther down on the gas pedal I had to strain my neck to see out the window over the steering wheel. I pressed more firmly on the pedal and watched the speedometer slowly move up to 60. Sixty miles an hour! I'd never gone that fast in my life. I had heard the phrase, "going like sixty!" and guessed that was pretty fast. We zipped across the Yolo causeway to Davis, slowed down through town, and then picked up speed again on the two-lane highway leading back to Woodland.

Dr. Noble said I drove very well—"Pretty fast for a boy of twelve!" I thanked him for letting me drive.

Y Camps

The YMCA was always fun. Starting at age seven I joined the Pawnee tribe of Friendly Indians and learned to say, "How!" while raising my right arm upwards (that meant, hello), and "Ahgenalia" (I think that meant, I'm fine). We boys got to know each other well, playing games and sometimes staying together overnight in a tent placed in the middle of the gymnasium floor, with poles sticking out the top like wigwams.

At age eight I was old enough to go to the YMCA summer camp up in the Sierras on Highway 50. It cost $10 for two weeks. Judge Chester McDonald, the father of my best friend Douglas, was taking a group of boys up, and I was to go with them. My dad promised he would come and get me the day camp closed.

Mother helped pack my clothes in a knapsack we bought especially for camp. She filled it with warm socks, underclothes, shirts, comb, toothbrush, pocketknife, flashlight with new batteries, mosquito repellent, and an extra pair of shoes for hiking. She slipped in some stamped penny postcards with our home address on them and instructed me to write something every day, telling her what I did at camp and how I liked it. Then she kissed me goodbye.

We piled into the Judge's big Buick and waved to Mother and Dad. I was eager to go, but there was a funny feeling in the pit of my stomach when the car drove off and I had to fight to hold back tears. I had never been away from my family before, except for the time I ran away from Grandmother Binkley.

The feeling in my stomach passed as we traveled out across the sweltering Sacramento Valley, up through the foothills, and on into the high Sierra Nevada mountains. It was exciting. Everything was new. The trees were taller, the woods thicker, the cliffs higher than any I had ever seen before. We passed a sharp-faced mountain called "Lovers' Leap." Doug's father told us it was named for an Indian girl and boy who were in love. The girl's father wouldn't let them see each other any more, so they went to the top and jumped off together, holding hands. That was sad.

At Twin Bridges Mr. McDonald stopped the car to let us lean over the bridge railing and watch the crystal clear water rippling over pebbles beneath us. Little trout were swimming together upstream. We looked up to see where the water below us came from. Way up above it flowed out of Desolation Valley and rushed down the mountainside. It didn't fall straight down like the ones I saw in Yosemite Valley but sprayed mist as it splashed over rocks. That's why they called it "Horsetail Falls." Finally we turned into a tiny dirt road, rumbled over a bridge, wound our way through a forest, crossed a meadow, and pulled into the YMCA campground.

The first thing in sight was a huge granite rock. On it was carved, in big letters, "I'm Third." I later learned that meant God is first, the other fellow second, and I'm third.

After lunch around large tables in the dining hall, we were assigned to our tents. Each held seven boys, all the same age, and a leader to teach and guide us and to keep us under control.

I don't remember much of what we did in the next two weeks except for making our beds neatly, cleaning the tents for inspection, and creating designs with small rocks and moss in front of the tent. It was especially fun to run through the woods a mile or so over to Camp Sacramento to play softball or row boats on the lake behind the dam. On the way we'd jump over logs that fell across the path, try to step around puddles in the marshes that grew "stink weeds," race each other to the next tree, and pick a wild flower to smell and put in a buttonhole while we skipped along. Every day I sent a postcard to my mother. They were short.

"I'm Third" was carved on a granite rock near the Sacramento Y.M.C.A. camp.

A Broken Promise

What I remember most was not the two weeks of camp, but the end of it. I was all packed up, ready to go home. My knapsack was filled with all my belongings (except for a shoe I lost), a booklet of camp songs that we sang at campfires, and a badge I won for jumping farthest for my size. Everybody's dad came to have lunch with his boy, sing songs together, and take them home. My dad didn't come.

I waited and waited for him. At three o'clock one of the fathers who arrived late to pick

Bob at Y.M.C.A. camp.

"Y" BOY TELLS OF CAMP LIFE WITH 'PROJECT'

1928

(By Scout Robert Nordyke)

Thirty-four of us arrived at the "Y" camp Saturday shortly after noon. We were billeted in three large tents of eight boys and a leader, and two smaller tents of four boys each with a leader in charge. Our tent leaders are Bruce Waybur, Louis Schlieman, Lorn Sachs and Lester Moeller.

The first night as usual was a noisy one, but Sunday was one that will long be remembered. Services out under the trees. Mort Wilson, General Secretary of the Sacramento Y. M. C. A. gave a wonderful talk about a crippled boy who learned to swim and saved another boy's life.

Then a lady with a beautiful voice sang and another lady played the camp organ. A Y. M. C. A. band from Sacramento played several pieces.

It sounded better than any band I have ever heard. Maybe it was because it was over 6000 feet elevation. They make us eat slower than we want to but give us all we want to eat.

Writing this is my camp project for the day. Mr. Howell gives us projects every day. One of the boys is making a deer out of moss and moulding it on the hillside. We are allowed five cents each day drawn from the canteen.

It's open now so I bette[...]

Y.M.C.A. camp song book.

*Bob's 1928 description of camp life
was printed in his town's newspaper.*

up his son said, "Bobby, you're the only one left. Why don't you come down to Woodland with us? We'll be home in just a few hours."

"No! My daddy promised he'd come to get me."

By late afternoon all of the kids were gone, and I was alone with a few leaders who were preparing for the next camp. They asked me to eat supper with them. I couldn't eat.

It got dark. My daddy still hadn't come. I couldn't stand it any more. I started to cry. I ran out into the woods, jumped across a creek, hid under some bushes, and fell asleep.

When I awoke it was pitch dark. I was cold and shivering. Remembering where I was, I didn't know what to do. Why hadn't my daddy come to get me? He promised he would. He doesn't love me any more. Maybe I'll have to walk home. He said he'd come and get me. Why didn't he?

It kept going over and over in my mind. Then I started to cry again, and dropped off to sleep.

It was daybreak when I woke up. Voices were calling from the direction of the camp. They seemed to be calling for me. So I walked back to the camp.

Louis Schliemann, my tent leader, saw me first. "Where have you been? We've been looking everywhere for you!"

"My daddy didn't come to get me. He promised."

"Come wash up and get some breakfast. I'll call your dad and see what we can do."

I didn't feel much like eating. Louis called my dad who told him that he got busy and thought someone else would bring me home. Dad called Judge McDonald, who was visiting nearby at Echo Summit, and asked him to pick me up and bring me home when they came.

Doug and his father arrived soon after that and took me with them to Tahoe City for the night. I quickly forgot about going home.

We all returned to Woodland the next day. My mother hadn't been worried. She knew someone would take care of me.

Every summer, from ages eight to twelve, I attended the same Sierra summer Y. Camp. It was always interesting and exciting, and I looked forward to it all year long. Each camp was different, and better, I thought—at least better than the first one. As the years went on, I was given more responsibility and became a sort of leader's helper, which made me feel important. They really needed me.

Prince

In the fall, winter, and spring of 1929–1930, early in the Depression, I worked at odd jobs to earn the $10 it cost to go to summer camp: mowing and raking other people's lawns, baby sitting, washing windows, and doing whatever work I could find. By spring, a few months before camp was to take place, I had earned $9.80 and had only two more jobs to go before the camp would be paid for.

Then came a special experience. The Griffith twins, Bill and John, who were my age, had a litter of beautiful German Shepherd puppies. I wanted one, badly. They cost too much for me even to think about. But as they grew larger, it was evident that one had a long bulge in the middle of his belly. They called it a "hernia." Knowing how badly I wanted a puppy, the twins gave him to me.

I loved that little dog. The name I gave him, "Prince," fitted him just right. He was playful and friendly, racing around our backyard in circles, putting his front paws up on me, licking my face, and racing off again. We put a gate across the driveway to keep him in, and Dad helped me build a doghouse that Prince had to share one time with a baby pig.

Then he started to eat less and less. His food was left on the plate, his ribs began to stick out, he didn't run any more. He just sat there, looking at me when I tried to feed him by hand. He wouldn't even drink water.

Something was very wrong. What could I do? Mother said I'd have to take him to a dog doctor, but that would cost a lot of money, and we didn't have it.

I made up my mind. I was going to take him to the dog doctor anyway. So I looked up in the phone book under "Veterinarian," picked him up in my arms, and carried him down to the dog hospital.

The doctor came out to see me in the waiting room, wearing a white jacket. He looked kind. He asked me what was wrong with my puppy.

I said, "My puppy is sick. He has a hernia. I'll give you ten dollars if you will fix him."

The doctor carried him into the back room. I followed and watched while he examined my puppy. He put him on a table and turned him onto his back. He tried to push in the soft part on his tummy but couldn't. He listened through his earphones. Then he turned to me.

"I'm sorry, Bobby. Nothing I can do will make him well."

I cried. Then I picked him up, held him in my arms, and carried him home. He died a few days later. My dad and I buried him at our ranch. On the cross above him was his name, "Prince."

Chapter Three

❦ DEPRESSION VIGNETTES ❦

I know there was a Great Depression in the 1930's because I've read about it in history books and saw television shows about the soup kitchens in Chicago, the marches on Washington, and the crop pickers in California hanging their legs out of open box cars. It must have been very difficult for millions of people. John Steinbeck's *Grapes of Wrath* made me intensely aware of the trials of the unfortunate families leaving their dust-ruined farms in Oklahoma, crowding all of their children and belongings into jalopies and trailers, bedposts and chair backs sticking out in all directions, moving to the Promised Land in California, and finding such appalling conditions after they arrived.

I lived through that Depression, but it didn't seem to bother me. Maybe I was too protected or too busy growing up to notice. Maybe I thought that was just the way things were. Maybe less can be as good as more.

But looking back, some things were different because of it. I came out the far end of the Depression believing you should work hard, save money, get a good education, help less fortunate people, be honest and trustworthy, and not expect something for nothing. Even Grandmother Binkley's perpetually expanding ball of string, that she kept saving for something, taught me a lesson I can't seem to shake.

For the most part I wasn't aware of the Depression. But in retrospect a few little incidents should have brought it to my attention.

Pee-Wee Golf

In 1930–31 pee-wee golf was the rage. At least five of these miniature golf courses erupted all over town, ranging from simple, inexpensive ones that charged five cents a round to quite elaborate ones that cost up to twenty-five cents to play all evening. They were open at night, enticing customers in with bright lights that illuminated the playing fields. Holes were designed to shoot the little white balls over narrow bridges, through rattling tin-lined tunnels, across obstructive mazes, and around angulated curves. Loudspeakers supplied cheery musical background, often interrupted by blaring announcements.

During the summer of 1931 the YMCA had a pee-wee golf competition. I made first team (three players) for the Pawnee Indian Tribe by coming in second out of seven. Our team was up against the Navajos, widely known to be tough and aggressive, eliminating everybody who crossed their path.

This night was the championship game—Pawnees vs. Navajos. Excitement was at fever pitch. We spent all weekend practicing putting golf balls over the gymnasium floor, ricocheting them at precise angles off the wall corners.

Then it suddenly occurred to me: the entry fee was fifteen cents, and I didn't have it. I ran home, dismayed. Mother didn't have it either. What will we do? The Pawnees will lose without me.

Aha! An idea, says Mother. Maybe Florence Hershey will agree to be your sponsor (Florence was a classmate of Mother's at Mills College and one of three maiden sisters who lived in a palatial green three-story home at the west end of Main Street, owned farmland as far as the eye could see, and had bought a new black Hudson car that could start just by turning the key). Mother bounced to the phone, rang Florence through the operator, and in a calm, sweet voice wondered if perhaps Florence could be a sponsor for Robert at the big competition tonight. Without him, the Pawnees might not be able to win.

To my glee, she agreed, right there and then, no questions.

Well, the game wasn't all that great. The Pawnees did win, but by the narrowest of margins, and not because of me. Anyway, we stopped the roll of the Navajos.

I thanked Florence for sponsoring me. She said she was pleased to do it.

Apricot Picking

The summer was hot, and I was out of school without a job. Nobody seemed to have one. During Dad's travels around to ranches trying to buy and sell sheep, he stumbled on something I could do—pick apricots at the Hennigan ranch at the south end of town beyond the city limits. The arrangements sounded reasonable: ten hours a day, ten cents an hour, with ten cents taken off to pay for a sandwich and the sweetened red water they provided for lunch. Work started and ended at six.

The pickers were a mixed collection. Schoolboys made up half the crew. The other half were a motley bunch of hoboes rounded up from shanties along the railroad tracks and brought to the ranch by truck. All seemed pleased to have a job.

The days were sweltering and the work was hard. Each picker was assigned his own heavy fifteen-foot wooden ladder that reached to the apricot-laden limbs and had to be re-set each time a branch snapped back after being cleaned of fruit. We clambered up the rungs to fill our buckets with soft, ripe apricots, hoisted loaded buckets down to the clod-covered ground, spilled them out over the drying trays, and then dragged the ladder on to the next limb and climbed wearily up. Rumor had it that the boss at the ranch house was watching us through his binoculars to be sure we were working hard enough. By late noon of the second day the muscles of my arms, neck, back, and legs were so tight and sore and I was so dead tired I thought I could never move again.

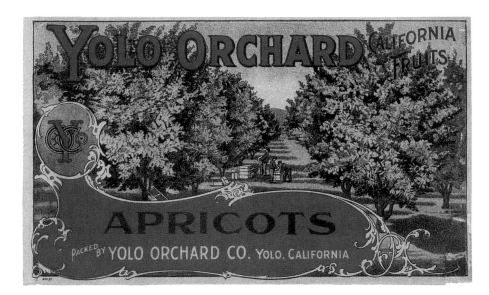

Apricot
picking

Saved by the ranchhouse bell! Out came the lunch on a wagon. But I was so nauseated from fatigue I couldn't eat. Instead, I stretched out in the shade of an apricot tree next to a new-found friend. He couldn't eat, either. Anyway, the sandwich wasn't very good, and the colored water was sickening.

An airplane was flying high above us, slowly passing, leaving a contrail in a thin line that feathered out behind, breaking into little puff formations in the distance. I remember well our conversation.

"You know what I'm going to be when I grow up?" I asked.

"I'll bet you'll be an apricot picker!" he joked.

"Nope! I'm going to be an airplane pilot like that fellow up there. Think about it. All he does is sit, driving his plane through the air, comfortable in a soft leather seat, glancing at the dials now and then, guiding it this way or that around a cloud, landing smoothly and taking off with a roar, really enjoying himself. Bet you he makes fifty cents an hour. What a life!"

The only mishap on the job came when I plucked off a juicy apricot that was being enjoyed by a honeybee. It responded by sinking its stinger into the meaty muscle of my hand. In the quick reaction of swiping the bee off, its plump stinger remained and I inadvertently squeezed it. Within minutes my hand puffed enough to make me the only one-handed apricot picker on the crew.

Lucky for me school started up again in three and a half weeks, because that's about all the apricot picking I could take. But I felt fortunate that I had a job at all. A lot of other people didn't.

The Lost Dime

It was Saturday afternoon. I was whistling my way up Second Street on the way to the matinee starring Tom Mix, wondering how the heroine would be saved this time, flipping my dime into the air to see how often it would come down heads. The dime somehow went askew and landed on the ground, nowhere to be found. I looked and looked, in the grass, on the sidewalk, in the gutter, over and over. Where could it be? Couldn't have gone that far. A small tear gathered.

It was almost two o'clock, time for the show to start. Only one thing to do—Mother would be able to find it or give me another. So I ran home. She was sewing in the front room when I arrived out of breath. There was no more money in the house at all, she said, so we'd have to find the dime or I couldn't go to the movie.

We both searched everywhere, even beyond where it was likely to be. Suddenly she spied a faint glitter. Wonder of wonders, the dime was standing on its edge between the lawn and the gutter. She found it!

Mother suggested that it would be better not to flip it in the air any more. I said I wouldn't.

Barber dime (left), 1892–1916, and Mercury dime (right), 1916–1945
The value of a dime:
10¢ = entrance fee to Tom Mix Saturday matinee
10¢ = payment for singing on Sunday with the Episcopal Church Boys Choir
10¢ = payment for picking apricots for one hour
10¢ x 100 = $10.00, or cost for two weeks at Y. Camp
10¢ x 100 = $10.00, or the cost for the veterinarian's care of a dog

Sanitary Dairy

ICE CREAM -:- FOUNTAIN -:- LUNCH

604 MAIN STREET
WOODLAND, CALIFORNIA
June 19, 1935

Letters of recom-
mendation

TO WHOM IT MAY CONCERN:

  The bearer of this letter, MR. ROBERT
NORDYKE, has been in our employ for sometime and
we are very willing to recommend him as a most
capable and conscientious young man, who is deserving
of the utmost confidence of anyone who may employ him.

  His leaving our service was deeply regretted
by everyone with whom he worked, and he carries our
best wishes for his success elsewhere.

    Very truly yours,

    SANITARY DAIRY

LD:HC   BY *Mrs S.L. Dole*

Lindsay, Calif.,
153 N. Harvard Ave.,
Sept. 17, 1934.

To Any One Anywhere:

  Should you be looking for a sane,
safe, capable driver for any car, we would like
for you to try Robert Nordyke. We had him drive
for us this entire summer in Santa Barbara, Calif.
He handled a big Nash 6 on congested highways, per-
ilous, narrow mountain roads with perfect ease and
safety, observing road conditions so we were at
all times comfortable and happy.

  We think him The Best In The West.

  Signed *N. S. Marshall*
   Mrs N S Marshall
 Martha Stark (Trained Nurse)

WOODLAND DAILY DEMOCRAT, WOODLAND, CALIFORNIA, TUESD

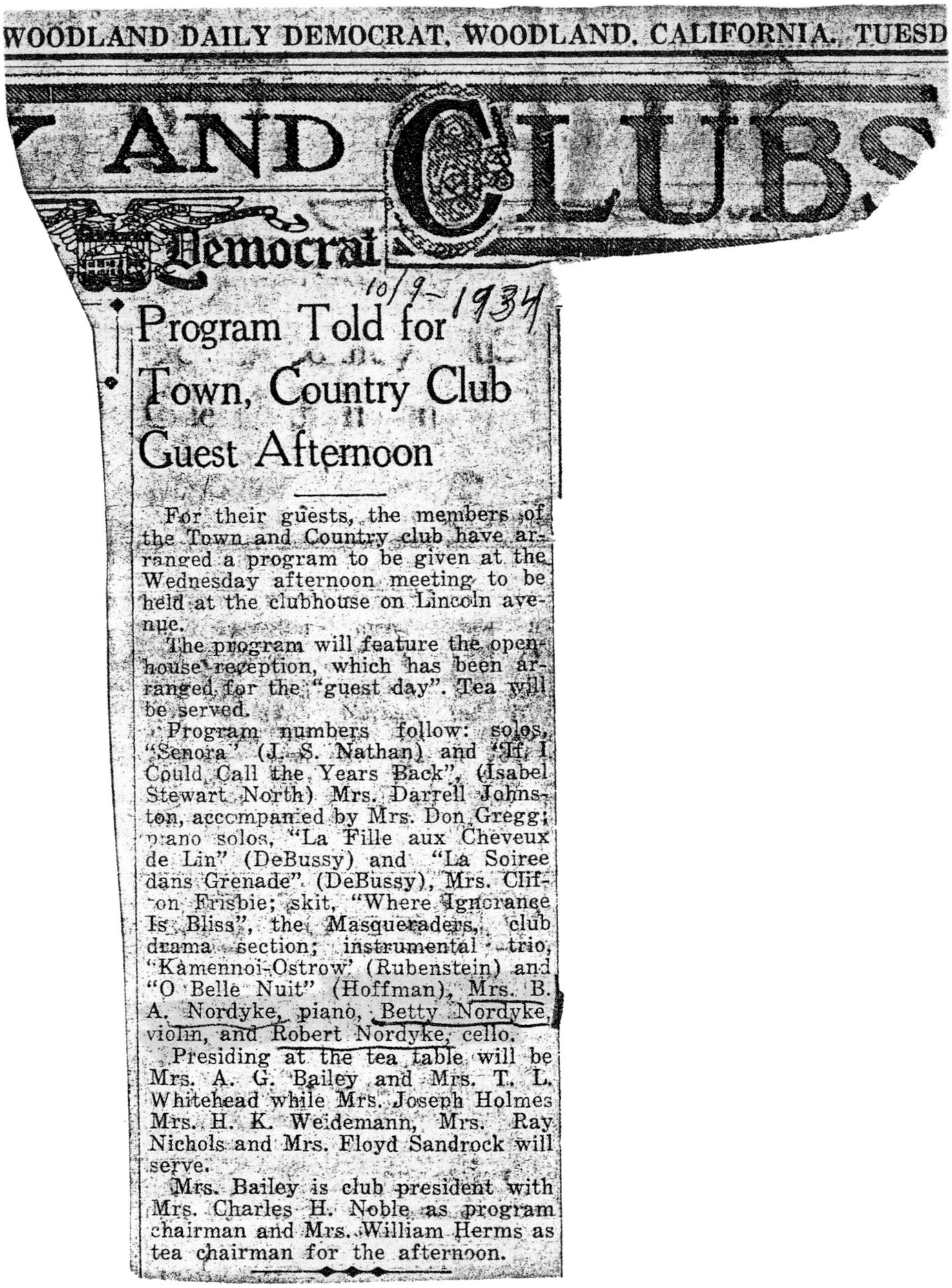

AND CLUBS

Democrat

10/9-1934

Program Told for Town, Country Club Guest Afternoon

For their guests, the members of the Town and Country club have arranged a program to be given at the Wednesday afternoon meeting to be held at the clubhouse on Lincoln avenue.

The program will feature the open-house reception, which has been arranged for the "guest day". Tea will be served.

Program numbers follow: solos, "Senora" (J. S. Nathan) and "If I Could Call the Years Back", (Isabel Stewart North) Mrs. Darrell Johnston, accompanied by Mrs. Don Gregg; piano solos, "La Fille aux Cheveux de Lin" (DeBussy) and "La Soiree dans Grenade" (DeBussy), Mrs. Clifton Frisbie; skit, "Where Ignorance Is Bliss", the Masqueraders, club drama section; instrumental trio, "Kamennoi-Ostrow" (Rubenstein) and "O Belle Nuit" (Hoffman), Mrs. B. A. Nordyke, piano, Betty Nordyke, violin, and Robert Nordyke, cello.

Presiding at the tea table will be Mrs. A. G. Bailey and Mrs. T. L. Whitehead while Mrs. Joseph Holmes Mrs. H. K. Weidemann, Mrs. Ray Nichols and Mrs. Floyd Sandrock will serve.

Mrs. Bailey is club president with Mrs. Charles H. Noble as program chairman and Mrs. William Herms as tea chairman for the afternoon.

The trio—Bob (cello), sister Betty (violin), and Mother (piano)—played music for an afternoon tea at the Town and Country Club of Woodland in 1934.

WOODLAND DAILY DEMOCRAT, WOODLAND, CALIFORNI
June 10, 1955

A 'Coed' But Not Sissy

Woodland Boy Works Way Through Mills College

Robert Nordyke, 15, of Woodland believed to be the only boy student ever to work his way through a girls' college. He's a student at the Institute of International Relations, a Summer session feature, at Mills College, strictly a girls' school. He walked from his home to attend the course preparatory to entering Stanford University.

He is the only male student ever to work his way through an exclusive girls' school.

And he walked all the way from Woodland to Oakland to do it.

The unusual student is Robert Nordyke, 15-year-old graduate of the Woodland High school and son of Mr. and Mrs. Byron A. Nordyke of Woodland. Robert is making his way through a course at the Institute of International Relations, now in session at Mills college, in order that he may be better prepared to enter Stanford university next semester.

"I plan to ean my way through Stanford and thought this would be good preliminary experience," Robert said. "I have specialized in history and government courses in high school and intend to make these subjects my life work," he added.

Nordyke is working his way through Mills college by scrubbing, painting, hoeing and mowing on the college campus.

In the morning, the boy attends courses and takes his notes. In the afternoons he dons jeans and becomes a manual laborer to earn the $25 tuition fee required at the 10-day institute.

"I much prefer the lectures to the hoeing and other work," Robert said.

". . . the only male student ever to work his way through an exclusive girls' school."

Betty & Bob

Betty and Bob used long skis in the snow at Pike City. The skis were "eleven feet long, narrow and heavy, made of oak. They were beauties! The poles were tall, reaching over my head, and heavy, with a disk near the bottom to keep them from piercing the snow too deeply."

Chapter Four

∽ PIKE CITY ∽

It was the worst of times, it was the best of times, depending on whose point of view you took. It was 1932, in the depths of the Great Depression, in the little Sacramento Valley town of Woodland, California, when we first heard about Pike City.

Dad had been the successful owner of the town's main meat market and the "Nordyke Building" on Main Street near Second that housed the butcher shop. Meat for the market came from our ranch where we raised and slaughtered hogs, sheep, and beef cattle. Our three hundred acre farm grew alfalfa, oats, wheat, and barley that helped to feed the livestock and provide income.

Dad was elected to the City Council and was, for a time, Mayor. From outward appearances he was prosperous, having owned a Willys-Knight and a Studebaker at the same time. He was medium height, somewhat feisty, protruding around the middle (reflecting his love of meat and potatoes), a family man, father of seven children, and full of confidence—until 1929!

Suddenly the stock market crashed and the Bank of Italy (the solid and impressive old stone edifice on Main Street) failed, taking with it whatever holdings we had. At age ten I remember working on our harvester, filling up sacks of wheat, covering my sweaty face with a handkerchief to protect against breathing the chaff, and being told that it cost a dollar to produce each sack that now had to be sold for fifty cents.

Within a short while, all of Dad's properties were lost. He walked up and down Main Street, looking for some kind of business. Often he would take me with him to go to farms where he acted as a middleman, buying livestock and selling them to large slaughter houses like Mace's in Dixon, collecting a commission without putting up any money. I remember standing behind him while he was pleading with Mr. Mace to take some sheep he had an option on. I didn't feel good about that.

As the Depression years went on, business became worse and Dad became somber. I overheard Mr. Johnson, who owned the grocery store, telling Mother that it was hard for him to extend any more credit to our family for milk. Even though it hurt Dad's pride to have Mother work to help support the family, he finally gave his blessing for her to try to get a teaching job. What else could we do?

That's when we heard about Pike City. Through the help of the placement service at Mills College (where Mother had graduated in 1913), a letter came from the Sierra County

Board of Education advising her that there was an opening for a teacher in Pike City. This "city" was a nearly abandoned gold mining town in the Sierra Nevada foothills, twenty-five miles north of Nevada City on Highway 49 (named for the 1849 gold rush days), and five miles out into the woods from the little village of Camptonville. Its population was about fifty persons within several miles. In order to qualify for an elementary school, nine students were required. Five children lived in the community, awaiting a teacher; with the addition of the four youngest children of our family (Betty age 15, Bob 13, Helen 11, and Jim 8), that made nine students who needed education. Magic!

Mother was ecstatic. "What fun we'll have!" she said. Dad was quiet. He agreed to take us up and settle us in, but he preferred to come back and stay in Woodland, where he belonged. Maybe he could make some money buying and selling sheep. We kids thought it would be an adventure going to a new place—in the mountains, in a little town, maybe even snow. What fun! Mother's eternal optimism was contagious.

The townspeople of Pike were to provide the new teacher and her family a house for $25 a month, unfurnished, sight unseen. "That sounds wonderful!" Mother said. Dad wasn't so sure, but he went ahead anyway and found a four-wheel trailer that we hooked on behind our old Willys-Knight car (Ed Leake, the editor of the *Woodland Daily Democrat*, who lived across the street, called it Technocracy, with an accent on the second syllable).

All of us pitched in and filled the trailer with a big load of what we'd need: clothing, beds, mattresses, dishes, silverware, chairs, tables. They stuck out every which way. Hidden inside, where nobody else could find them, were each child's special belongings: a worn blanket, a tattered doll, an old collapsible fishing pole. Mine was a hunting knife in a scuffed leather sheath to protect me from mountain lions, if there were any.

The Trip to Pike

Early next morning, after tying our sleeping bags onto the running board, Dad, Mother, and three of the kids climbed into the car. I stayed out and performed my usual job of cranking the engine to get it started, then jumped in. As we moved slowly down the driveway, the load felt heavy, and Dad kept it in low gear until we reached the highway.

By late afternoon we had crossed through the steaming Sacramento Valley, climbed the Sierra foothills, followed Highway 49 through Grass Valley and Nevada City, and arrived in Camptonville. We crawled out, stretched, and talked to an old mountaineer who lived in the last house before starting off down the dusty road to Pike.

"Why would you want to go *there*?" he asked in disbelief. "Nobody lives there! The road is steep and rough. It goes for a mile down to Oregon Creek, then up a mile and a half to the top (hope you don't meet anybody, no room to pass), then along a winding road through the woods, and finally you'll find it—if it's still there."

The family moved from Woodland, across Sacramento Valley, to Pike City—"a nearly abandoned gold mining town in the Sierra Nevada foothills."

As an afterthought, he added, "It's getting a little dark now, but try it if you want. Might be better to wait until morning."

Dad decided to go now.

The next fifteen minutes I'll never forget. I was sitting in the front seat. Dad was driving. He turned down the gravel-covered dirt road past a sign that said, "Danger. Seven percent grade." As we moved ahead he put on the two-wheel brakes. The rear wheels locked and slid in the loose gravel, pushed on by the heavily loaded four-wheel trailer.

Turning to Mother and the other kids, Dad ordered, "Jump out!"

Without a moment's hesitation, they jumped out.

"Bob, you stay." I stayed, but kept the door open.

We moved relentlessly down the hill, rear wheels dragging. I leaned back and pressed my feet hard against the floorboard. It didn't help.

*Camptonville, where the
family went for supplies
and where sister Betty
attended high school, is
a little village five miles
through the woods from
Pike City.*

*Wilson's Log Cabin in
Camptonville served as
the general store, the post
office, and the gas station
for residents of Pike City.*

Then I saw a frightening thing in front of us: the road took a sharp turn to the left, bending back on itself, and straight ahead was a steep cliff. The turn was too sharp for us to make with the trailer pushing from behind.

Dad shouted, "Jump!"

I jumped, rolled over on the ground, sat up. In horror I watched the car and trailer sliding down the hill with Dad in it. He stayed with the car, holding down the brakes, still sliding. My heart was pounding.

I yelled at the top of my voice, "Dad—get out!"

Just as he reached the corner, he swung the wheel hard to the right. The heavy car and trailer crunched to a halt. He had driven into something that I hadn't noticed—a small tree at the edge of the road, the only thing that could have stopped him from going over the cliff . . .

After that, we all jockeyed the car and trailer back and forth, put rocks under the wheels so they wouldn't slide, inched around the corner, aimed down the road, and got in. At the bridge over Oregon Creek we stopped to rest, with a sigh of relief and wonderment of what would come next.

The pull up the other side was slow. At the steepest point the car chugged to a stop. Not enough power. All of us kids climbed out and pushed, keeping the car and trailer moving to the final turn that led onto the nearly level hogsback. The sun was setting behind us as we drove along the winding road through the forest towards Pike.

House to Home

I must have fallen sleep. When I awoke the next morning I was lying on a mattress, covered by a blanket. I got up and wandered around in the old mountain house. The place was bare. A living room without chairs but with a blackened stove in the middle, a sleeping porch with broken screens above where the others were still in bed, no electric lights, a kerosene lamp in each room, a wood stove in the kitchen, a sink without water, cobwebs in every corner. Where was the bathroom?

I pushed open a creaky screen door that led onto the back porch where wood was piled high, corded against the wall. From the outside the brown, unpainted house looked run down like a haunted house in Saturday matinees. Fifty yards down a worn trail was a little shack without windows. A quarter-moon was cut through the door. Inside I found what I thought might be there—two holes side by side with a deep pit below, a Sears Roebuck catalog with torn pages, a faint unpleasant aroma—our "outhouse." I used it.

Up another path was the well. The structure above it was in disrepair. Two-by-fours came up from the sides, and between them hung a rusty iron bar. Suspended from the center of the bar was a pulley, threaded with a frayed rope. One end was attached to a

*Our house
at Pike
City in
1933.*

*Our house at
Pike City in
1996, including
the outhouse
(below left)
and the well
(below right).*

heavy metal bucket, the other disappeared down the dark hole. I dropped a pebble and heard a splash. I figured it would be my job to supply water for the family.

When I returned to the house there was a lot of commotion going on. Everybody was up, looking around. Like Christmas. Mom thought it was wonderful. Dad was dismayed. It wasn't worth $25 a month. It was only an abandoned miner's house. How could anybody live in such a thing? Anyway—first things first—let's get busy and clean it up.

It wasn't long before the house became a home. Beds, tables, chairs, desks were moved in from the trailer. Cobwebs were brushed away. The fire in the living room stove was filled with kindling and wood from the porch and lighted with matches that we found in the cupboard. The whole house became clean and warm. We started up the kitchen stove to cook the meals and heat the water in a big tub that was later set on the kitchen floor each Saturday night so we could take baths (whether we needed them or not)—cleanest one first, usually the girls.

The Well

The next thing we needed, Dad said, was fresh water. I was to be his helper. Together we walked along the path to the well and pulled up bucket after bucket of heavy, murky water. Finally there was no more water, but a lot of mud was left at the bottom that had to be cleaned out. Here was the plan: he'd drop me down on the bucket, I'd fill it with mud, and he'd pull it up. I'd stay down until the well was cleared of mud and then he'd haul me up.

So I straddled the bucket and swung forty feet down into the dark, with my legs and back hitting the sides alternately. I filled load after load full of the heavy mud, scooping it up with the edge of the pail first and finishing each one off with cupped hands until the well was almost dry and the bottom felt hard, like sand. Dad called down to tell me to sit on the bucket and hold on to the rope. He pulled me up.

Next day we went out to see if fresh water had seeped into the well. As we cranked the first bucket-load of water near the top, the frayed rope snapped and the metal hit the bottom with a sickening thud. What if the rope had broken yesterday?

School

The school was not far from our house: down a steep hill a few hundred yards to the creek, across a small bridge, up the other side a short distance, and onto a flat that contained the school building. I thought it looked like a country school ought to look—white, square, with a front porch and a bell tower. On the side was the playground with swings, bars, and tables. Beyond, a dam held back the creek water, high enough for diving but intensely cold, even in summer.

The Pike City School "consisted of one big room. In the middle stood a pot-bellied stove."

The inside of the school consisted of one big room. In the middle stood a large pot-bellied stove. The students' fathers (except for mine, who was always away in Woodland) kept us supplied with wood. In the fall and winter it was my job to fill the stove each morning and keep the fire from going out during the day. On cold days all nine of us kids would back up to it, wiggling sideways for space. Sometimes my pants would get so hot I couldn't sit down.

Mother had to teach all of the elementary school classes at the same time. I don't remember how she did it. Children in each grade level were put into a corner so they could work together without bothering the others. Each student had a desk with a built-in inkwell. I took English, history, and math.

I think I worked especially hard to please the teacher but she gave me mostly B's for grades. When I took the Sierra County-wide examinations, I got 99% in English composition and 96% in math. Mother explained the difference: she didn't want it to look as though she was favoring her son.

The Accident

There is one memory of Pike City that still causes me to suddenly, almost convulsively, break into tears. One hot summer afternoon I was standing on the schoolhouse porch when I heard the frightened call of a little girl saying, "Come help Mama! Come help Mama!"

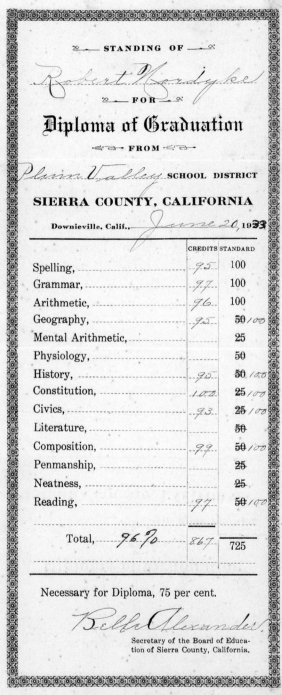

STANDING OF

Robert Nordyke

FOR

Diploma of Graduation

FROM

Plum Valley SCHOOL DISTRICT

SIERRA COUNTY, CALIFORNIA

Downieville, Calif., *June 20*, 19**33**

	CREDITS	STANDARD
Spelling,	95	100
Grammar,	97	100
Arithmetic,	96	100
Geography,	95	~~50~~ 100
Mental Arithmetic,		25
Physiology,		50
History,	95	~~50~~ 100
Constitution,	100	~~25~~ 100
Civics,	93	~~25~~ 100
Literature,		~~50~~
Composition,	99	~~50~~ 100
Penmanship,		25
Neatness,		25
Reading,	97	~~50~~ 100
Total,	96.70	867	725

Necessary for Diploma, 75 per cent.

Bell Alexander

Secretary of the Board of Education of Sierra County, California.

Bob's diploma from Sierra County.

She grabbed my hand and we ran together along the dusty road, on and on until we came upon an overturned car in a shallow gully. The driver's door of the old open-topped Ford was lying across her mother's chest, and white foam bubbled from her mouth. The little girl's grandma was sitting on the ground beside the car, moaning, "Why couldn't it be me? Why not me?"

I tried to raise the car door, lifting, pushing, shoving with all my might. It didn't budge. I looked for a lever, found none. I told the little girl to run home as fast as she could to get her daddy or somebody to help. She ran. I tried to lift the door off Mama's chest again and again. It didn't budge. Grandma kept moaning, "Why not me?" Mama didn't look at me when I touched her face. Her eyes stared straight ahead.

It was half an hour before the little girl came back with her daddy and two other men in a truck. Together they raised the car door off of Mama and pulled her out. She didn't respond. She was dead. The men put Mama, Grandma, and the little girl in the back of the truck and drove off. I wanted to walk home.

The funeral was in a house, since there was no church. A small organ accompanied the father, his children (our best friends and schoolmates), our family, and others from the community singing "Nearer my God to Thee."

I always felt that the little girl's father thought I hadn't done enough, or quickly enough. He didn't say so, but I felt it. Should I have run to get him as soon as I heard his daughter calling for help at the schoolhouse? Should I have been able to lift the car off of his beloved wife? I am haunted still.

Snow

In December a wonderful thing happened. Looking out the window we saw big, fluffy snowflakes floating down, landing on the windowsills, turning the bushes white. Maybe we could ski to school!

Up on the rafters of the old barn near the house we found two pairs of skis. They must have been used by an old-timer going cross-country between his mines, I thought. One pair was eleven feet long, narrow and heavy, made of oak. The other pair was shorter, wider and lighter. They were beauties! I liked the long ones. The poles we found with them were tall, reaching over my head, and heavy, with a disk near the bottom to keep them from piercing the snow too deeply. There was a hard leather strap about three inches wide in the middle of each ski to keep your feet in place. I tried them on.

Mr. Robinson, a plump retired neighbor with a bald head, came over to help us with the skis. There was one pole for each person, he said. You pushed yourself along with both hands on the pole. The ski bottoms were scarred and needed smoothing. He helped us find some tar. We heated it over a fire, spread it on the bottoms while it was still hot,

Icicle from 3 to 4 feet long.
January '33 sonds
Betty
Our House the day we shoveled it '33

Children, snow, and icicles decorated the roof of the Pike City home.
Captions written on photos in 1933 by Bob's father, Byron A. Nordyke.

and rubbed it hard and long with soft cloths, like they did in the old days. It made them slick. Then we rubbed on wax we found in Mother's jelly jars. The only trouble was, there wasn't enough snow on the ground to try out the skis.

But then it came. It snowed and snowed. It covered the ground, the trees, and the house. Only the tops of the fences stuck out. Snow was high against the windows. Old-timers said it was the deepest snow in anybody's memory. Teacher and students couldn't get to school. Fathers of the students came to our house and shoveled a trench that went all the way down to the creek and up the other side to the schoolhouse. Walking along inside we could barely see out.

After school I'd often put on the skis and slide quietly out through the woods alone, stopping to look at the fresh tracks of birds and squirrels and foxes and deer, listening and looking intently for the animals that had made the tracks, occasionally startled by limbs of fir trees snapping back into place after snow dropped off, warmed by the sun. I remember saying quietly to myself the lines my mother taught me from Robert Frost:

> Whose woods these are I think I know,
> His house is in the village though;
> He will not see me stopping here
> To watch his woods fill up with snow.

And, looking back towards our mountain home as the woods began to darken, a poem of Wordsworth:

> It is a beauteous evening, calm and free;
> The holy time is quiet as a nun
> Breathless with adoration . . .

Early one Saturday morning I put on my skis and went up the mountainside, way up to the top, farther than I'd ever been before. The snow was deep, the sky was clear, the air was crisp. I leaned against my ski pole. My eyes wandered over the vista, down the other side of the mountain, across the ravines, through the woods. The mountains were covered with tall trees, with smaller ones and white open spaces beneath. They went on and on into the distance, fading into the mist like Japanese paintings.

Ho! What's that? Smoke was wafting in a spiral from the top of a little house in the distance. Somebody must be there—nobody else within miles. How could anyone live so far away? I'll go for a visit. So I tightened my ski straps and took off down the hill, slipping across ice beneath the trees, and coming to a skidding halt in front of the gate, spraying up snow.

A gruff voice called out, "Who's there? What are you doing here?"

"My name is Bob. I've skied over from Pike," I answered somewhat timidly.

"My name is Bob, too. Bob Beam."

His voice softened. "Come in! I haven't seen anybody for months. Are you hungry? Want some flapjacks?"

"Sure!"

The small log cabin was unpainted. Some of the chinks between the logs were broken and patched to keep out the cold. A high chicken-wire fence around it was designed to keep out deer. Inside the cabin it felt warm and smelled of food cooking. Four solid oak chairs were positioned around a small table covered with torn oilcloth. There was only one table setting, but the tall, lanky, middle-aged, bearded miner quickly pulled a plate out of a cabinet and a knife and fork from a drawer and set a place for me. The kitchen stove crackled. A big iron frying pan was warming up.

"What month is it?"

"December."

Bob throws a snowball.

"What day is it?"

"The twentieth."

"What time is it?"

"Nine thirty five."

He adjusted his watch. "I've been here for three years, mining gold in a shaft behind here. The house and mine were abandoned fifty years ago, so I moved in and took it over. Don't think anybody owns it. Nobody comes to visit. Glad you came."

Mr. Beam went on to tell me how much he liked being alone, how he had a little garden where he grew carrots, peas, and corn. Trouble was, the deer would jump over his fence and eat the vegetables. Now and then he'd shoot a deer for meat. Once every few months in the summertime he'd start up his old Chevrolet truck and drive the back road to Downieville, turning in his gold to the County Assessor's office to get money to buy butter and flour, sugar and salt, seeds for his vegetables, matches for his fire, and a few shells for his 30/30 rifle. When the snow came, like now, he couldn't get out at all. Then he'd work in the mine and read some old newspapers left over from last summer. What could be better than that?

What I liked most were the flapjacks. He'd pour the batter into the heavy frying pan, and when it was ready to turn, he'd hold the handle with both hands and throw the half cooked flapjack high into the air. It would turn lazily, just enough to land with a light splash on the pan. He'd wait until it was done enough on the other side, shake it a little, and flip it again, not quite so high. This time it would land on a metal plate on the table. I ate two, covered with butter and with sugar-water for syrup. Best flapjacks I ever tasted!

Mr. Beam picked a coal oil lamp off the table and we walked out to see his gold mine. It pierced into the mountain just behind the cabin. We had to lean over to get through the opening. The old railroad ties that were meant to hold up the sides and the top were watersoaked and sagging. Some were broken and had fallen down, so we had to step carefully over them. Water dripped from the walls and ceiling.

As we walked farther in, the tunnel darkened and his voice sounded like an echo. He lit the lamp. At the end of the tunnel lay the pick he used for breaking rocks off the walls, and the shovel he used to put the rocks into a bucket to carry them outside. He told me that out in the light he broke the chunks with a heavy hammer and looked closely for streaks of gold. The mining companies broke up the granite with big, heavy, expensive "stamps" that were pulled to a height by a gasoline engine and then let fall. His way was better. He did it by hand.

We went back to the gate. I put on my skis.

"Goodbye, Mr. Beam. Thanks for the breakfast. I liked seeing the mine."

"Goodbye. Call me Bob. Come back whenever you can."

I skied off up the mountain and down the other side to Pike before anybody missed me. I never saw Bob Beam again, but many times since then I've tried to flip flapjacks in the air. They never tasted as good as those I had in the snowed-in, isolated miner's cabin.

The snow kept falling. One beautiful night, when the moon was full, all of the kids in the neighborhood decided to ski in a large open field that sloped down towards the main road. We went up sidewise, then whooped off the top as fast as we could, straight down or criss-crossing the slope, sometimes holding hands in twosomes or threesomes, occasionally getting tangled, falling, laughing.

The memory that lingers most is my last run off the hill, heading down to the right towards home. The moonlight erased the shadows, and at full speed I whacked into the top strands of a barbed wire fence that I didn't see at all. Only a few feet of it emerged above the snow. The sharp barbs cut through my Levis and drew blood that trickled into my socks and shoes. I still have scars on both legs, left over from an otherwise wonderful night of skiing.

Ski jumping was a favorite sport. All of us got together and built a little upsloping wooden structure with a four-foot dropoff and shoveled snow on top of it. We walked our skis up the steep hill towards the post office, strapped them on, and used the single pole to push off as fast as we could down the well-worn track and over the jump. We landed in the middle of the snowpacked main road, sometimes upright, sometimes sprawling out of control. We competed to see who could jump the farthest.

When snow was deep, no cars moved, but the U.S. Mail Service had to get through. The mailman, Mr. Espinosa, came to our rescue—not only for mail, but also to carry us to Camptonville to buy and bring home our "provisions," or, on Mondays, to take sister Betty and Lola, the oldest Chatfield girl, to Camptonville for advanced classes. He was a short, jocular, mustached Portuguese man who lived with his family just outside of town. Each morning we would hear the jingle of the harness bells as his horse trotted up the hill towards our house, drawing a sleigh behind. Mr. Espinosa sat on the front board seat next to a whip that stuck straight up in the air. I never saw him use it. The horse wore a single pathway in the snow, and the iron sleigh runners slid along on either side. He would stop by in the morning to see if anybody needed to go to "town," and he passed by in the evening before he urged his tired horse up the hill in front of our house to the post office.

Christmas

Up to this year, we kids somehow let Santa Claus know what special things we wanted for Christmas, and (if they didn't cost too much) we usually got them. This Christmas was different. Mother's monthly salary was $125. After paying for rent, food, and clothes for all of us and gasoline for Dad's car, there wasn't much left over. In November, on one of his occasional trips up to Pike from Woodland, Dad announced that each of us could have just one Christmas present, to be chosen from the Sears Roebuck catalog. That's all. Make your choice wisely; you won't get anything else. No more than $10 each.

We pored over the thick catalog. I don't remember what Betty, Helen, or Jim picked, but I knew exactly what I wanted. The catalog opened easily to the right page (I had looked at it many times before).

I gazed with fascination on the pages with pictures of leather boots. There were short

Bob with his parents on Christmas day in the snow in front of the Pike City house.

ones coming just over the ankles, higher ones that came part way up the lower legs, and very high ones coming up above the calf. That's the pair I wanted—there! They had a little leather rim around the toe. Laces went through holes at the bottom and around clasps above so you could put them on fast when you got up in the morning. And they were very high—eleven inches, it said. They would make me look like a miner. That's what I wanted. Nothing else.

Dad didn't think it was a good idea. Out in the snow and the puddles they would leak through and make my feet cold. You should get some rubber boots to keep your feet dry, and wear warm socks inside, he argued.

No! I wanted those leather boots. I'd put on some neat's-foot oil to keep them from leaking. Dad finally gave in.

Three days before Christmas a big box with my name on it came in the mail, with Sears & Roebuck on the outside. What excitement! I could hardly wait to put them on.

We cut a small fir to make a Christmas tree and put it in the living room. It didn't have lights or tinsel, but that made it "natural," Mother said. In the morning we had to eat breakfast before opening packages—a tradition at our house. I finished quickly, and peeked into the living room through a crack in the door.

There was my box, big as day, still in its package! Dad and Mom were unusually slow finishing breakfast, but when the go-sign was given I rushed in, picked up my package, and took out my sharpened hunting knife to cut the tape that held it together. Somehow the blade slipped and sliced deeply into the palm of my left hand beneath the index finger. The process of opening Christmas presents had to be delayed until I washed the blood off in the kitchen sink, pulled two pieces of tape crosswise to hold the skin together, wrapped the hand in a clean cloth, and raced back to the living room.

The little accident didn't stop me from quickly opening the package with one hand and putting on the beautiful, tall, leather-smelling boots. I slipped my feet into them. My toes didn't reach far enough in, but I knew they would fit perfectly as soon as I added a couple of pairs of thick socks.

It turned out that Dad was right. When I went out in the snow my socks got wet and my feet were cold, despite how much oil I added to the leather. I never told Dad that. But I liked them anyhow. I looked like a miner. It was the best Christmas I ever had.

Summertime

The snow left the ground, a blanket of grass and flowers came wondrously up out of nowhere, and my feet warmed. Then the grasses dried and dust covered the roads. We walked the five miles to Camptonville every week to buy groceries. Mr. Hecton at the town's general store would put the food packages into my knapsack, being sure it didn't weigh more than thirty or thirty-five pounds.

"It isn't good for a young fellow to carry too much weight," he warned, and then waved as I'd start off with the pack on my back, whistling down the steep road (where we almost went over the cliff on the first day of our visit to Pike).

Thick dust covered the road. There were no tire tracks, only fresh deer tracks and single undulating lines left by snakes crossing the road. The snakes must have pushed back and forth sideways as they moved, making little wedges in their tracks, first to the left, then to the right. Flocks of wild pigeons were startled out of madrone trees where they were eating red berries.

The bark of manzanita bushes glistened everywhere. Tall pines with yellow plaques, silver and red firs, and cedars reached for the sky above me. The cedar limbs often had a sudden change of direction; after a few feet at right angles to the ground, they turned straight upwards again, as though they had to go around something. Why didn't I see any snakes when there were so many tracks? Maybe they were curled up in their holes because it was too hot out here. There was plenty of time to wonder about things while you were walking along, kicking little rocks in the dust, spirits high, on the road to Pike.

Mountain Lion

One early Saturday evening I left the Camptonville store with staples packed high in my knapsack, walked down to Oregon Creek and up the other side, and turned up the ridge towards home. The road ahead was gently winding, with tall trees close at hand on either side, leading over the brow of a hill.

Something at the very top startled me: a big animal was outlined against the sky, crossing the road. It was too small for a deer, too big for a dog, larger than a wildcat but looking like one. A long tail followed him, longer than his body. Probably a mountain lion?

I was glad I had my hunting knife. I took it out of the sheath in my belt, checked its sharpness by running my thumb along its edge, and held it in my hand, shaking slightly. I didn't know what to do with it, but it made me feel better. Should I turn around and go back to Camptonville, or keep going towards home? Would the mountain lion still be there, or would he be gone? Was he afraid of me? Was I afraid of him?

I walked straight ahead, slowly. Near the top of the hill I stopped and listened. Mountain lions, somebody had told me, made sounds like a baby crying, leading you towards them when you shouldn't go. I listened carefully but couldn't hear any sounds. I walked forward a few yards more. There in the dust in front of me were the largest tracks I had ever seen. Like a cat, but they seemed bigger than my whole hand.

Let me out of here! The next three miles through the woods were the fastest I ever walked, often looking over my shoulder as the road darkened behind me.

Next day, Sunday, a truck came by with a State emblem on its door. The driver was in a uniform and said he was a mountain lion hunter for the State. There had been reports of some in the area, killing deer without eating them. He wanted to know if we had seen either any injured deer or any mountain lions. I told him I thought I saw a mountain lion on the Pike side of Oregon Creek the evening before. He thanked me. We never heard anything more about it.

Jealousy

It must have been Easter vacation. Mother wasn't teaching, so several times she accepted an invitation from Mr. Campbell, a County road supervisor, to ride along with him in his quarter-ton truck to help him check the roads in Sierra County.

"That sounds like fun," Mother said. "There's no school now, and I can visit parts of the County I've never seen before."

It fitted her way of thinking—to see and learn about some new thing.

Mr. Campbell was about Mother's age, rather plain, lean, tall, clean-shaven, quiet spoken, with a jutting jaw and a Meerschaum pipe that curved below his chin, reminding my brother Jim of Popeye. Several times that week he picked her up in the morning and brought her back in late afternoon.

At supper she told us about the wonderful trips they took around Sierra County to check on the work crews and to be sure that slides from the heavy winter snows had been cleared from the roads. She wrote to Dad in Woodland and told him about it, too.

In the evening a few days later, Mother came to me in distress. She had received word that Dad was driving up that night. He was very angry. She wanted me to sleep with her, to be with her when he came. A .22 rifle was kept in the closet of the house. She asked me to hide it. I picked up the gun and hid it under some straw at the back of the barn. Then I climbed into bed with her on the screened porch, leaving my clothes on, ready to meet Dad when he arrived.

Late at night I heard the Willys-Knight screech into the yard. Jumping up, I went out to intercept Dad before he came into the house. He still wore his hat, which seemed odd, and looked angry. He wasn't smiling, and he didn't say hello to me. At first he just sat there in the car. I opened his door. He still just sat there. I remember even now my awkward words (I couldn't think of anything else):

"Take off your hat and stay a while."

"Don't get fresh with me, Robert." He called me Robert when he was annoyed with me.

He slowly stepped out of the car. I moved next to him and walked with him to the house. Mother met him at the door. She didn't know what to expect. Dad began to talk loudly as they moved into the living room. I retreated to the porch. I could hear Mother's voice occasionally, low in the background. That went on and on. I tried to stay awake so that I could protect Mother, but I couldn't keep my eyes open on the dark porch, and finally I must have dropped off to sleep.

Mother and Dad at Pike. "Take off your hat and stay awhile!"

On the next morning Dad seemed more like himself, but quieter. He said hello to me and the other children, and he put his hand on my shoulder, as he sometimes did to show his affection. It seemed that he was trying to apologize in his own way for the night before. We had a light breakfast together that Mother cooked.

Mother didn't go out for rides any more with Mr. Campbell. I saw a different side of my dad than I had seen before.

Air Shafts

Scattered here and there through the woods behind our house were holes in the ground that I later learned were vertical shafts dropping deep down—maybe three or four hundred feet—to connect with horizontal mine shafts and provide the miners with air. The openings had been crisscrossed with small poles cut from pine trees, covered with brush. But that was fifty years ago. The poles now were rotted and broken, and they looked stronger than they really were.

We kids would stand at the slippery edge of an air hole, peer into the dark chasm, and toss in a rock. One game was to listen intently and count how long we could hear the rock go tink . . . tink . . . tink . . . fainter and fainter, one-thousand, two-thousand, three-thousand—and try to figure how deep the hole was.

We never considered that the game might be dangerous.

Epilogue

On May 10, 1992, which was Mother's Day and, coincidentally, my mother's birthday (she would have been 103 years old), I had the sudden urge to return to Pike City, even though I knew "you can't go home again." My wife Ellie, her brother Ralph, his wife Susan, and I were having brunch in South Lake Tahoe. I suggested we run over to Pike, 120 miles away, and visit it—for fun. To my surprise, they agreed.

We planned to enter the Pike outback by way of the Camptonville road in memory of the car and trailer trip that nearly ended in catastrophe; however, it was closed, we were told, by disuse and slides.

We then re-routed ourselves on what used to be the back road to Pike, into the mountains from Highway 49 along the Middle Fork of the Yuba River. It turned out to be a wide highway, newly paved and curving through beautiful wooded mountains on the way to the little gold mining towns of Forest (5 miles) and Allegheny (8 miles). (This was the same road along which my sister Betty and I skied cross-country from Pike to Forest, 60 years before, for the fun of it, a distance of 12 miles over a narrow, unpaved, snow-covered road. By the time we got home the leather foot-straps on my 11-foot skis had produced rows of blisters across the tops of both feet. Probably Betty's, too.)

Now, though, it was a paved highway. After five miles or so we turned into a side road with a sign and an arrow: "Pike. Population 140. Elevation 3,300 feet." That's a lot of people, I thought. Where are they?

Two miles along, the road opened into the remains of what I remembered as Pike City. The route from there to Camptonville was closed off. The road that led down to the creek and up to the schoolhouse had huge blackberry bushes on both sides, just like before. On the open flat, where the schoolhouse should have been, towered powerlines with a little powerhouse beneath. The "pole line" that I knew still cut a swath through the woods.

We drove along the road that led past the powerhouse. It was covered with dust and pinecones, and appeared unused for years. This was a shortcut to the town of Forest. (Along here the little girl ran to get help for her mama.) I decided not to continue any farther.

Returning to the main street, only three old houses remained. One was ours. It looked pretty much the same, but it was smaller than I remembered. The outhouse was still standing, with a quarter-moon cut in the door. I peered in to confirm the two holes and the faint smell. Nearby stood the well. A pulley hung from the center of a rusty iron rod, threaded by a frayed rope attached to a wooden bucket.

Roadsign to Pike City. Bob, with grandson Andy Cozzette, revisits Pike in 1996.

Up to now we saw no living souls. Where could they all be? It was getting dark and we had to leave, even though we had talked to no one. Driving out of town we noticed a sign on the entrance to a side road that we had overlooked. The word "Elysium" was made out of fresh flowers, with a heart on top. I turned in sharply, and we found a cemetery that I didn't remember at all.

A lone man was fixing flowers and pulling weeds around his wife's grave and around his own, too, although his final date was not yet inscribed. He introduced himself as Norman. He had moved here ten years ago because it was quiet. "Few people; that's good," he explained. His wife had died four years ago. She was young, in her early fifties, but age, he commented wryly, is not one of the criteria for entering a graveyard. "Look— over there is a one-year-old."

We told him our mission: to see what had happened to Pike in 60 years. "A lot of things have changed," he said. "A few years ago a fire swept through the area, burning up most of the houses, many trees, and the schoolhouse. The post office is still there, though." It was a different one than I remembered. Mr. Robinson, who helped us with our skis, had died.

The group of graves over there, so neatly kept, with flowers, whose are they? The Chatfields, he said. My heart thumped and blood left my face. After a few moments of recovery, I explained to Norman that the Chatfields and our family made up most of the school in 1932. I thought they were in Calaveras County. No, he said, they all came back here—home.

The large grave in the middle said, "Hawley Chatfield, 1890–1985." He was the father, head of the family. On his right lay Rose, Hawley's first wife and the mother who died in the auto accident when the little girl ran up to me and called, "Help Mama!" "Died September 15, 1932." A flood of memories welled up in me as I stood gazing at the grave, numbed. I hoped no one noticed. Hawley's second wife was buried on his left, and preceded him by several years.

In the next grave was Lola, 1917–1936, eldest daughter of Hawley and Rose. Several years older than I, classmate of sister Betty, full of joy and verve, electrocuted by a bathtub heater in her prime. I thought back on the faint smile she gave me from across the room at her mother's funeral. I couldn't help paraphrasing a poem by Wordsworth:

> She lived unknown and few could know
> When Lola ceased to be;
> But she is in her grave, and oh,
> The difference to me!

It was nearly dark. No more time for memories. We drove back to Lake Tahoe silently.

Robert A. Nordyke, age 16, Roosevelt High School graduation picture, 1935, and letter of recommendation, 1941.

OAKLAND PUBLIC SCHOOLS

ROOSEVELT HIGH SCHOOL

OFFICE OF PRINCIPAL

OAKLAND, CALIFORNIA   December 27, 1941

To Whom It May Concern:

Robert A. Nordyke was graduated from Roosevelt High School in June of 1935, and received his A. B. degree from the University of California, four years later.

I have known Robert and his family very intimately for years, and although I have had hundreds of young men under my supervision, never have I had a finer, a cleaner, and a more deserving young man than Robert Nordyke, for they "just don't make them better".

Robert made a fine record in school and college, and was a deep and thorough thinker, analyzing a problem from all angles and arriving at a carefully thought out solution to the problem.

Robert is a natural born leader of men, and has always received the heartiest of support and co-operation from those under his leadership, inspiring in them a deep respect for his ability, and confidence and a deep faith in his power to meet any situation which might arise.

He leads in an unassuming manner which compels people to trust him and lean upon his power and strength. He seems to possess an uncanny ability to find a way out, no matter how tight a hole he may be in, and also inspires those with him to place full confidence in his ability to solve the problem. His inspiring leadership ability is very marked, and even the most disgruntled, soon learn to trust and respect him and to accept his judgment.

Seldom does one find a young man with such fine moral standards as Robert has. He possesses no bad habits of any type and is as clean and fine as they come.

Robert gives the best there is in him to give, (and he has much ability to give) and whoever secures his services will have no regrets.

I can recommend Robert Nordyke as the "finest of the fine".

Sincerely

Neva M. Brodrick

Neva M. Brodrick
Counselor

The Sacramento Box and Lumber Company mill at Kyburz, California in 1939.

Chapter Five

◐ SUMMER OF '39 ◐

Timber!

It was late spring of 1939. At age 19 I was just finishing my junior year at Berkeley. Milton Lott, who lived in the same boarding house and was editor of the UC campus literary magazine, asked if I wanted to take a job in the woods during the summer. He knew I was barely making my way through college by working in the University Library four hours a day and hadn't been able to save any money. He had heard of a job that could take on two students felling timber in the Sierras up above Sacramento. The pay was good (a dollar an hour plus keep, better than the thirty-five cents an hour I earned at the Library) and it should be fun—good change from sitting and studying, too. If things went well, maybe I wouldn't even have to work during my senior year and could concentrate on my courses.

Sounds great! Let's go!

So Milton arranged for us to take the job. The day after my last final examination, I said goodbye to my mother, dad, sister Helen, and brother Jim in our home on Majestic Avenue near Mills College, jumped on the streetcar to the Greyhound depot, met up with Milton, and caught the bus for Sacramento. From there we were transported along the winding and increasingly beautiful Highway 50 into the Sierras and were dropped off at Kyburz, a little village that was just a widening in the road with a store and service station at the 4000-foot elevation level. I dropped a nickel in the pay phone and asked the Sacramento Box and Lumber Co. camp office man to come and get us.

Half an hour later a lumber truck slid to a halt beside the station. The bearded driver called to us, asking if we were the new loggers. We nodded, and he beckoned us to hop into the cab with him. We bounced across a little bridge over the Silver Fork of the American River, up the other side on a rough dirt road for several miles, and arrived at an encampment of tents in the log-scarred forest—our home for the summer.

The timber boss, a bulky, raspy-voiced fellow with scuffed leather boots, met us at the truck and offered to show us around. Over there was the mess-hall where we'd eat, the dormitory for our cots (they supplied blankets), the outside toilets, and the trucks that took the crews and equipment to the field. Workers were expected to rise at 5:30, eat breakfast at 6, and jump onto the trucks at 6:30. They were allowed half an hour for lunch, with the day ending at 5:30. Whistles would give us the signals.

Off to the side while he was talking huge Caterpillar tractors crawled over the hillsides picking up fallen logs, snaking them down the steep slopes to the roads, leaving deep gashes in the soft earth, and placing the logs in stacks on long trucks that would carry them to the sawmill.

"That's it, boys. Rest up tonight; you'll be hard at work tomorrow," the boss advised. That sounded good. We were eager.

Next morning at 5:30 a shrill whistle echoed through the dormitory. We jumped out of bed, put on our Levis, heavy socks, leather boots, and long-sleeved plaid working shirts, and trudged over to the breakfast hall. About forty rough, unshaven men sat around big tables in the mess hall. Some of them grunted a greeting to us over the clanking dishes and silverware, but most of them just hunkered over their plates without looking up or nodding recognition.

Promptly at 6:30 a beat-up, tan, flatbed truck pulled up in front of the mess hall. On command, fifteen of us clambered onto its hard, slippery surface, bunched together, and

"Huge tractors crawled over the hillsides picking up fallen logs snaking them down the steep slopes to the roads, leaving deep gashes in the soft earth, and placing the logs in stacks on long trucks that would carry them to the sawmill." Photograph courtesy of Randy Leffingwell (Leffingwell 1997:22).

bounced along in the cool morning breeze up a steep, winding, pot-holed road. We were dropped off at the equipment shack. There the sawyer kept the newly sharpened saws and double-bladed axes on the walls in rows, a name on each. Ours were already assigned. The timber boss called out, "You two will work together. Grab your saw and axes. Don't touch the trees circled with green paint; they're good timber. You'll be cutting down snags, marked with red. This is Forest Service property. The foresters do all the marking. They tell us which trees we can take for lumber and which snags we have to cut down and burn. Part of the deal."

Snags, it turned out, are dead trees, usually killed by beetles. Most are obvious, with big, dead branches and dry bark segmented into sheets ready to fall at the touch of an axe. In common lingo the loggers called them "widow-makers." We were told to keep an eagle eye upwards while felling them, especially at each impact of the axe. Some snags looked healthy, but the very top was dead, meaning the whole tree was dead. Many snags were five or six feet through and a hundred feet high.

We had to learn about felling trees pretty much on our own, although the field boss started us out. First you decide where you want to lay the falling tree. Then you carefully estimate its lean to see whether it will go where *you* want it to go or whether it was likely to go where *it* wants to go. There has to be a compromise. Once decided, a quarter-diameter undercut is made with the seven-foot two-man saw at right angles to the direction of fall.

Back and forth we went, Milton on one end, I on the other. Fresh curls of sawdust came out with each slice. It took some time to smooth out our sawing technique so that one let go exactly when the other pulled. During the learning process we got a lot of laughs over our awkwardness.

When the sawed undercut was finished, the axes came out. Each of us had timber fallers' axes, sharp as razors, with cutting edges on both sides. We'd sink them into the tree alternately, angled downward. With every stroke a big chip flew into the air. Always we kept a vigilant and anxious eye out for falling limbs and bark. When the chopping was finished, we'd move to the opposite side and start the saw swinging again, back and forth, back and forth.

Then came the fun. Nearing the finish, the tree would creak and groan and begin its fall. We'd bet on where it would land, hopefully within a few feet of where we aimed it with as little damage to other trees as possible. Now and again the tree would crash precisely on a stake we placed in the ground for a bet, and we'd let out a whoop! If we were on the side of a steep slope and the tree was large, it would lift itself off the base and catapult down the mountainside, coming to a sliding stop thirty or forty feet away from the stump, spewing dust and branches and bark high in the air.

Occasionally a flying squirrel entertained us. On its uphill route it would climb to the top of a tree; then, with legs outstretched and skin pulled taut, it would push off and sail thirty or forty yards downward to the base of a higher tree and repeat the process. Traveling downhill was a beautiful sight to see. The squirrel would climb to the top of a tree, take advantage of the ever-receding slope, soar lazily downward for several hundred yards, and land under a tree with a thud.

We worked for a month, hard. Our hands were calloused, muscles firm, weight down. It felt good. The boss sometimes brought cold beer in the middle of a hot, sweaty afternoon.

I got to know Milton Lott well. He was 6'3", lean, always with a faint smile set off by his blond mustache, full of humor, somewhat slow moving, muscular, observant, thoughtful. We worked well as a team, especially after we got the knack of sliding the saw smoothly without vibration. Each of us wielded the axe equally well left or right handed, so we could trade sides to reduce fatigue. He told me about his boyhood on his family's farm in the Snake River Valley outside of Idaho Falls where he milked the cows, drove the team, raked the hay, planted peas and tomatoes. The summers were short. They could grow only one crop of alfalfa, and it wasn't very good at that. He commented that it was difficult to get enough hay to feed the animals through the long winters. That was hard, I said, compared to my dad's farm in the Sacramento Valley where we had three lush crops each year—until we lost the whole farm early in the Depression. Milton was especially interested in Indians. He wrote well. Professor George Stewart at Berkeley once wrote that he "displays as promising a talent as has appeared in this generation." He had submitted the first chapters for a novel about buffalo and Indians called *The Last Hunt*, and received a literary fellowship award from Houghton Mifflin to complete it. The novel was finished after he graduated from college.

A Worker's Union

One evening a group of men came to our dormitory wanting us to sign up for a workers' union, the Carpenters and Joiners. It sounded good to us. Both of us had taken political science courses and had thought a lot about unions. I once wrote a paper on the laws that were put into place as part of Roosevelt's New Deal in the early 1930's including the National Labor Relations Act that protected union rights. So we signed.

Next morning at breakfast a man from the administration hut read off a list of 18 names. It included Milton and me. WE WERE FIRED! Now! Get your things and leave! That shook us up. We looked at the list. Every person who signed to join the union the night before had lost his job. Nobody else.

We left. No choice. We gathered our few belongings, boarded the Greyhound at Kyburz, headed to San Francisco, and went straight to the National Labor Relations Board, explaining that we thought employers couldn't fire us just for joining a union. They agreed. Two weeks later we received nice letters from Sacramento Box & Lumber telling us that we were re-hired and that they would be pleased to have us return to work. A check was enclosed to cover retroactive wages and any inconvenience the company may have caused us. How nice!

All eighteen of us arrived back at the logging camp the same day, and were signed on again. After a good night's sleep, Milton and I jumped on the morning truck, rumbled up the road, picked up our saw and axes at the sawyer's shack, tramped into the woods, and started to cut down snags, chuckling to ourselves over our good fortune.

Within a week every man who returned was fired again, this time individually, for "not working hard enough." We thought there might be a principle here to fight for, but we desperately needed to get on with making money to finish our senior college year.

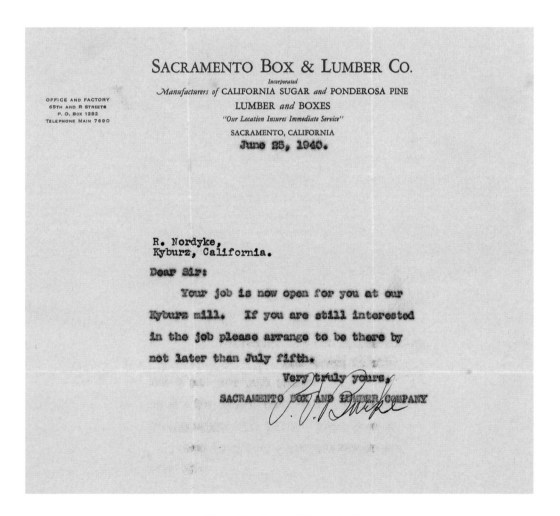

The rehire letter. "How nice!"

What else could we do for the remaining months of summer? Milton suggested we go to his family's farm in Idaho. We could pitch hay, milk cows, or get some kind of work. They were always looking for people to help. Sounds fine! Especially since no other jobs appeared on the horizon to improve our meager financial situation. Milton got the OK from his family to come up.

Trainyards

Working in Idaho sounded exciting. I checked it out on a map. Idaho was one thousand miles away—over the high Sierras, across the Nevada desert, over the huge Salt Lake to Ogden, and north over low mountains to Idaho Falls near the western border of Wyoming.

How would we get there? Three choices: go by bus (no money), hitchhike (tight laws and hard to get rides in the desert), and "ride the rails." Milton had ridden in boxcars before and thought that would be the most practical.

"OK," I said. "Let's try the train!"

A freight train in the San Francisco Mission Street railyard. Photograph by courtesy of Bill Yenne.

My mother thought the idea of working on the farm was better than cutting down timber, especially after I told her about the "widow makers." She was less than enthusiastic about our riding in boxcars but I thought it would be safe enough, and fun, too. That was good enough for her.

We packed our belongings in small bags containing the same things we took to the lumber camp. I added a black wool short-coat because Milton said it got very cold at night, even in summer. The coat was to be my "saving grace" later on. Each of us put ten dollars in our jacket linings. Then we jumped on a streetcar and headed for the Oakland rail yard, expectations high.

At the yard there were dozens of freight cars, some hooked together, some standing alone. The tracks were crisscrossed in mazes. Which one to Sacramento? We were confused, but quickly we met up with others who were going the same direction. Most were itinerant field workers, traveling from one fruit picking job to the next, in groups. These men were relatively clean and friendly and invited us to share an open boxcar with them. A few were "hoboes," just traveling about, alone, no special destination in mind, carrying tattered packs with open tin cans hooked to the outside that were smudged from warming coffee on open fires. We quickly learned to stay away from them.

Our new friends were full of information. The trip from Oakland to Sacramento and on to Roseville, they said, was easy. The railroad managers understood that migrant workers had to move about to help the farmers at picking time. Nobody would bother you. But if you're going "over the hill" across the Sierra Nevada mountains, watch out in Roseville. That's where they attach the cars together. They add an extra big steam engine in front to pull and another on behind to push. There won't be any open boxcars, so you'll have to ride on top. It can get pretty suffocating when you go through long tunnels. The railroad "bulls" (armed guards hired by Southern Pacific) don't like bums riding trains out of Roseville, so you may have to hide and jump on after the train starts moving.

That was more information than we wanted. We pulled ourselves into the boxcar just as the train started up. The trip through Sacramento to Roseville was easy. Thirteen men sat on the floor of the car with us. The door was open, so we sometimes dangled our legs over the side, getting a continuous stream of fresh air and an expansive view of the countryside—green with alfalfa, irrigation ditches flowing into the fields, telephone poles ticking past. The ride was bumpy. Often we'd lie on the floor, but oddly the steady rocking and clicking of the rails didn't give us any rest. Approaching Roseville, we were advised to jump off before the train came to a stop, make ourselves scarce until the new combination of engines and cars clanged together, then climb aboard after the train started for the trip over the Sierras. We followed their instructions and jumped off.

WASHINGTON

MONTANA

Missoula

IDAHO

OREGON

Boise

Idaho Falls

Ogden

Winnemucca

Salt Lake City

Reno

Sparks

NEVADA

UTAH

Sacramento

Berkeley

San Francisco

Oakland

CALIFORNIA

*Map of the route of
the summer trip by
"hobo" train, hitch-
hiking, and bus.*

——————— train

– – – – – hitchhiking

·············· bus

Over the Sierras

The reorganized train began to move out of Roseville. From our vantage point behind a train on a siding, we watched for open boxcars passing by, but found none. So we chose the nearest closed car and grabbed onto the iron ladder between cars to keep as much out of sight as possible. The train lurched and groaned as it picked up speed towards the mountains. As soon as it was well out of town, we climbed on up to the top.

A narrow walkway led us along the wobbly crests from car to car. Men were already lying on the first one we came to, and on the next one too, so we treaded cautiously and erratically along the tops, jumping between cars in response to bursts of click-clack from the rails. Finally we found a car without anyone on it, where we could be by ourselves. Here we settled down on the center walkway for the long and (we hoped) exciting ride ahead. The train slowed perceptibly as it rocked its way higher into the mountains. The air began to cool, so I put on my wool short-coat, which made me comfortable and warm.

Then came our first tunnel. Off to the side appeared a rectangular white sign with bold black lettering saying, "Tunnel length, 400 feet." Within seconds the cars ahead disappeared into the gaping black hole and we followed. Smoke poured out of the engine and enveloped us. By the time we were inside the tunnel it was completely filled with black, thick smoke. I began to choke. Tears poured from my eyes. I tried to hold my breath but the tunnel was too long. I took out my clean white handkerchief and held it over my nose and mouth. That was better. Then we suddenly burst out of the smudgy black hole and I gulped fresh, pure air. Marvelous!

As we chugged on into the mountains we tried to hold our breath through fifty-four tunnels, each with a sign telling us its length, ranging from one hundred to twelve hundred feet. At last the mountainous terrain receded, and there were no more tunnels. The train gathered up speed as it rolled, in darkness, out onto the flats leading into Nevada.

The Bull

It was midnight when we jerked to a wrenching stop in Sparks, Nevada, the railway connection for Reno. Both Milton and I were half starved, having had our last bite of food two days before in Oakland, although we had found water in Roseville. We flipped a coin to decide who would get off and buy food for both of us. I won the toss. So I climbed down the ladder to the tracks and started to walk in the direction of town, alongside the cars, stumbling in the dark.

Within a short distance I nearly collided with a huge man in a dark suit. I asked him for directions to the closest store where I could buy some food.

"My friend and I are hungry," I explained.

"Are you from this train?" he asked. By this time I recognized him as one of the rail-road bulls I had been warned about.

"Yes."

"You're not going to any store. You're coming with me!" He pulled out a shiny-barreled pistol from under his coat and pressed it against my chest.

"Turn around! Walk! That way!"

I turned around and paced alongside the train. A quarter-moon was out, and the crossties on the track were barely visible in front of me. I walked faster, glancing back at him now and then over my shoulder. He began to get farther behind. Over on my right I noticed an open field full of high reeds, nearly up to my neck. The bull was even farther behind. I decided to make a dash for it.

I raced fifty yards straight out into the field and quickly hunched down. My heart was pounding. I wiped the cold sweat off my forehead. I kept as quiet as I could. My breathing sounded loud.

Minutes passed. A bright light beam passed back and forth over my head. I heard the crunching sound of boots along the track.

After a time that seemed forever, there were no more lights. No more sounds. My train began to move. The whistle blew its startup sequence, two longs, a short, and a long, that I had learned meant we're headed out. I waited until it gained enough speed, then came cautiously out of the reeds, furtively looked both ways, ran alongside the rumbling train, grabbed the cold iron ladder with my hot sweaty hands, and hoisted myself up the rungs to the top.

It was the wrong car. I balanced my way along the wooden walkway, jumping from car to car in the dark, until I found Milton. He was concerned, hungry, and waiting for food. After my story, he drew on his infinite patience.

"We'll get us some food at the next stop," he said.

Sparks, Nevada, train stop.

Winnemucca

Hours passed before we jerked to a clanking stop in Winnemucca. It was a little railroad town out in the middle of the Nevada desert. The time was noon, two and a half days since our last bite of food. The railroad track passed near the town, and we could see stores lined up beyond the tracks on the far side of a street.

The decision this time was to stay together. We would buy bread and milk. That should satisfy us for a while. So we climbed down off the train, jumped across the tracks, crossed the street, and proceeded rapidly to a store with a sign above it: GROCERIES. We walked in, picked out a loaf of bread from the shelf and a quart of milk from the cooler, laid them on the counter, and slapped down a silver dollar.

The unfriendly clerk pushed the groceries aside and said, "You can't have them."

"Why not? We have money. See?" We pointed to the silver dollar.

"You're dirty bums. We don't sell to bums. Get out!"

Looking at each other's faces, having come through the Sierra tunnels, and even though we felt faint from hunger, we could, at least partially, see his point. We picked up the dollar and reluctantly left the store.

The officious clerk in a second grocery store wouldn't sell us any food, either. "We don't sell to bums. Get out of here! Now!"

We were persistent, out of pure hunger. At a third shop our treatment was a little more civil. After some argument we were referred to the manager who explained his problem to us: "There are lots of hoboes getting off the freight trains here. They come across the tracks to get food. They're dirty, like you. They don't have any money. They steal. They're a problem for town people. At least you have money and you don't exactly look like hoboes. I'll let you buy some food, just this once. Take your bread and milk and get out of my store, quickly, before my other customers see you."

So we picked up the loaf of bread and the quart of milk off the counter, pocketed the change, left by the back door as directed, and settled down on the gutter of a side street. We broke the loaf down the middle and took alternate gulps from the bottle of sweet milk. Food never tasted so good! But before we finished, a shiny blue car with flashing red lights came up directly beside us, with two police officers in it.

"Get in!" one of them ordered. We got in.

"Which way are you going, east or west?"

"East."

"The train leaves at 1:15. You'll be on it." And we were. The police officers dropped us at the edge of the depot. At exactly 1:15 the starting whistle blew. Again we climbed to the top and found an unoccupied walkway. The train moved on towards Utah. At least our hunger and thirst had disappeared.

Nevada Desert to the Great Salt Lake

The train rumbled eastward. It picked up speed across the Nevada desert. Despite the breeze generated by the moving train—probably fifty miles an hour—it was hot. The heat, together with the steady droning and shaking, made us always tired. Sleep seemed continuously irresistible, but no matter how long we slept we were never rested. The narrow walkway we lay on hour after hour was uncomfortable. If you pulled up your legs, even a little, you'd be off the wooden strip and onto the sloping metal roof. That could be dangerous.

A new thought occurred to us. Why not move down to the side of an oil tanker? In Winnemucca we had noticed a narrow board running around these round black cars, about a foot wide, just above the wheels. Our fellow-travelers often seemed to choose those cars, settling down at the corners. Maybe you could lie on your side, bend your knees, get more rest?

So we picked up our belongings and walked precariously along the walkways, jumping across from one car to the next until we came to a round, black oil container with nobody on it. Letting ourselves down its side by an iron ladder, we groped for the firmness of the wooden runner under our feet, inched along it sidewise, leaned inwards against the tanker since there was nothing to hold on to, and settled down at the front corners. I took the left one, Milton the right.

The clicks of the wheels were much louder here (we were not more than four feet off the rails), but the ability to bend our legs up as we lay sleeping made it more comfortable than up on top. Looking across at Milton on the rare occasion when I woke up from a deep sleep, I could see one of his arms hanging over the side. Rather near the grinding wheel, I thought, and then went back to sleep.

As night came on, it became increasingly cold. Despite my short overcoat I began to shiver. Colder and colder! We agreed that we had to do something about it before we froze, so we moved to the top of the nearest boxcar. This wasn't such a good idea, either; it was just as cold, and the wind whipped the car sideways.

Then the thought struck us. Most of the boxcars carried fruit and vegetables and had to be kept cold. At both ends of each car were "reefers," deep, narrow slots usually filled with ice to keep the car contents cold. Most of them were locked closed, but some were open. Maybe one was empty.

Milton had scrounged a box of matches somewhere. We walked along the top of the boxcars in the dark, balancing the best we could. Each time there was an open slot we'd light a match and look down inside. All we saw were big blocks of ice, again and again. Not a place to sleep. After a dozen or more of these, and getting increasingly discouraged, we found one without ice. Eureka!

But a strong odor emanated from it. Lighting another match and looking more closely, we discovered the bottom filled with—what was it? Onions! Sticking an arm down inside, it felt warm. Choice: smell bad or freeze? So we helped each other drop down into the car, curled up on top of the onions, and fell fast asleep.

Next morning when I awoke there was an unusual, pungent smell about me, almost overwhelming. Then I remembered. Onions. Looking straight above through the reefer slot, the sky was blue and bright. I glanced over at Milton. He was awake, too. With a single mind, we rose to escape our smelly retreat. He cupped his hands together and hoisted me up to the top. Then I reached down and pulled him up after me.

What a feast for the eyes! We were out on a trestle above the Great Salt Lake. White salt on all sides, as far as the eye could see. The sun was just creeping up over the horizon. A pink glow emanated off the white crystal blanket in the east.

But it was the air that I remember best: soft and warm. You could almost touch it with your hands. And the smell! Never has man inhaled such wonderful, sweet air!

Ogden to Idaho Falls

Ogden was a major center for changing railways. We had been warned to watch out for "bulls" here—they were tough. We took care to keep ourselves scarce by jumping off the train long before it came to a stop. By this time we had enough experience to easily find a northbound train that was headed to Idaho Falls and the Lott family farm.

Our new transportation source was a short train—an engine and seven boxcars. One of the cars was open. We leaped on as it started to roll. Looking around on the inside we saw eight other people: four hoboes, with tattered packs and tin cans; two boys about our age, college students headed home; and a young man with a girl. The girl interested me because it was the first time we had seen any girl riding the trains since leaving Oakland. She wore a short, pink, rumpled dress. An orange ribbon partly controlled her blonde, unkempt hair. Sweat rolled off her forehead making rivulets across her dirt-smeared cheeks.

The train moved rapidly along the winding, narrow gauge track. It was the worst ride we ever had, wobbling and bumping with sharp turns. This went on for six hours. The girl and her companion backed themselves into a corner, leaning against the wall, carefully separated from the rest. She appeared increasingly tired and sullen. They had no food. One of the students moved towards her and offered half of his sandwich. Her companion motioned the student back, menacingly.

"Keep away!"

The student retreated to his corner.

As we pulled into the freight yard at Idaho Falls and slid off onto the ground, my last image of the girl remains in my mind even now. Her boyfriend was standing protectively next to her in the middle of the track. She reached for a handkerchief from her purse, wiped her smudged face, took out a silver-covered lipstick holder with a small mirror, and carefully applied red lipstick to her dirty lips.

The Farm

The little town of Idaho Falls was clean and bustling. Through its center coursed the Snake River, swirling over the falls that contributed its name. We walked around the middle of town for an hour or so. Milton was excited to return to the place of his boyhood, and he showed me his favorite haunts.

By nine o'clock in the evening we started to walk to the farm, several miles out of town. The sky was steel-gray and bleak. It was still light; we were far north.

Trudging along with our backpacks, we finally reached the long dirt road leading in to the farmhouse. The terrain was flat, broken only by willow trees lining the Snake River as it meandered through the countryside. Off in the distance to our left was a beacon light, turning around every minute or so, flashing over our heads as it passed. That was a signal, Milton said, beckoning to us. It always reminded him of home.

As we neared the farm gate, a whoop went up, and everybody came running out to greet us: Father Lott, who looked very much like Milton, tall and wiry, quiet-spoken; Mother Lott, who looked the part of a farmer's wife, slightly plump, full of smiles, with rough hands; a sister, sixteen years old, quite lovely I thought (Milton had warned me to stay away from her); and a 20-year-old brother, looking like Milton, too. I was introduced to each one, and we were eagerly urged to come in.

First thing we needed, Mother Lott said, looking us up and down, was a bath. Maybe it was our dirty faces and tangled hair that made her think of that. Or maybe there was an aroma left over from the onions. A bath sounded wonderful!

She handed me a towel and soap, a clean pair of pants, and a shirt, and promised to wash our clothes in the morning. Then I indulged in one of life's special pleasures—soaking in a deep, long bathtub with warm water up to my chin! It took me some time to wash off the dark ring around the tub afterwards. Then it was Milton's turn.

When we came out, fresh and clean, Mother Lott greeted us with warm home-made bread, baked that day; fresh milk from the Swiss cows in the barn; fresh potatoes, peas, and carrots from the garden; beefsteak from a yearling; and, for dessert, cream pie. What a spread for hungry boys!

For two weeks both Milton and I worked on the farm, driving the team, pitching hay, picking peas (they were delicious eaten raw, directly out of the pod), and doing odd jobs. It was evident to me, though, that the Lotts had plenty of helpers for the farm chores, that their funds were limited, and that I wasn't really needed.

One day I read in the local newspaper that the forests up in western Montana near Missoula were unusually dry and that lightning was starting dozens of fires. Men were wanted to contain the blazes. Both Anaconda Copper Co., which had large timber holdings there, and the U.S. Forest Service placed advertisements for firefighters. So, after consulting with Milton and his family, I decided to leave the comfortable farm and go it alone. After a final clothes-wash and another refreshing bath, I shouldered my knapsack, waved goodbye, and headed for Missoula to search out my fortune.

The easiest way to get there was to hitchhike. It took only three rides to arrive at the outskirts of Missoula. I was dropped off on the roadside by a farmer who was turning into his farmhouse lane. It was dark, and I was getting cold. I didn't want to spend money for a room, so I found a large billboard next to the road, bundled up beneath it, covered myself with my short-coat, and went fast asleep.

Fire!

Next morning I walked to the Missoula town center. There were dozens of men—maybe hundreds—lined up in front of the offices of Anaconda Copper and the Forest Service, hoping to be chosen as firefighters. Chatting with several men my age, I learned that Anaconda paid seventy-five cents an hour, the Forest Service fifty cents. The Forest Service had better equipment. Otherwise there wasn't much difference. They sent you out to the fires for a week or ten days at a time. You slept in tents on mattresses at the base camp. When you were out in the field, fighting fires, you slept on the ground, under trees, wherever you could, rain or shine. They provided a raincoat that slipped over your head and a rainhat. Grub was good if you were near the base mess truck; out on the fires they brought water and sandwiches.

When you came back to Missoula, the paymaster paid you in cash. We were advised to watch out for that. Sometimes guys were "rolled." Strangers could take money out of your hands, quick. The best way is to send it home by a post office money order.

It was late afternoon. I joined a line with about fifty others on the street in front of the Anaconda office. The line didn't move, but men filled in behind me. Then a representative came out and told us they were closing for the day but would open again at eight the next morning. Loud groans! I decided to hold my place in line by sleeping on the sidewalk that night, along with a lot of others. Glad I did, even though it was cold, hard, and generally uncomfortable, because when the line moved at eight o'clock the next morning I was the last person they signed up for the day.

The trucks that brought us out to the fire line reminded me of those at Sacramento Box & Lumber, but the personnel hauler was more comfortable—benches all around the sides and two down the middle. Two equipment trucks carried the gear and provisions we'd need: saws, axes, stove, collapsible toilet, tents, food, water. Our caravan of trucks bounced down a highway for twenty miles, turned off on small dirt roads another ten, then off through the woods where there was hardly a road at all. From an opening on top of a ridge I could see a fire in the distance, flames flaring and smoke billowing.

At last we reached the base camp, our home for the next ten days. It was in a meadow, still lush with green grass and tiny yellow flowers, with a crystal clear stream meandering through it. The view from there was beautiful. The mountains were gently rolling and deeply forested with huge trees, mostly Douglas fir, stretching on and on into the distance. There were fewer snags and the land was more densely covered with big trees than in the Sierras, I thought.

Not far away two fires were belching smoke; occasional tongues of bright fire leaped up and then retracted. The wind was light, blowing away from us. We were told to be careful if the wind reversed itself. It could crown, leaping from treetop to treetop, faster than you could run.

Big, dark cumulus clouds developed over towards the fire. Thunder rumbled in the distance and came closer. Lightning flashed, and a drenching rain poured down. It happened fast. My short-coat, which was only partly rain repellent, got soaked before they handed out the pullover raincoats. We rushed to put up our tent, quickly hoisted the center pole and slipped inside, leaving the pegs till later.

The thunderstorm passed as quickly as it came, and the sun was warm. We climbed out of the tents and helped to set up the kitchen on back of the truck, dig a hole and erect the plastic outhouse over it, and pound pegs into the corners of the sleeping tents to hold them steady in the wind. My short-coat was wet and musty-smelling as I hung it on a limb to dry.

We moved out before noon, on foot, and worked alongside big yellow Caterpillar tractors that were out in the field already. They were clearing brush and small trees in a wide swath in front of where the fire was expected to go. Our job was to quickly cut down larger trees within the clearing that were too big for the Caterpillars to push over.

All of this was done in the hope that an approaching fire would be contained. That assumed that the flames would be small enough to be stopped by a strip two hundred feet wide, that the wind wouldn't be strong enough to jump across it, and that the fire wouldn't crown. In that case, nothing could stop it. Small biplanes flew back and forth across the fire, streaming anti-inflammatory fluid out behind them. You could see the helmets and goggles of the pilots sticking out as they flew past, close to the fire.

After explaining my experience felling snags in California, I was assigned to a two-man saw team along with a short, bulky older man experienced in fire fighting. Another six saw teams were given the same assignment. Others were supplied with axes to chop down brush and pull it out into the center of the clearing. If the fire began to crown, we were on our own: go down wind and get out!

Off we started, single file. I carried a seven-foot saw over my shoulder. It wasn't long before another thunderstorm brewed. That might help to put the fire out, I thought, but I was concerned that the steel on my shoulder would attract lightning.

CRACK! Thunder roared, lightning flashed, a tree was split fifty yards away. I threw my saw to the ground. Later I laughed to myself about that. It was a reflex that had no sense at all. If the lightning hit me, it would have done so already. Throwing my saw to the ground couldn't help.

Twelve hours a day we cut trees as fast as we could. Information radioed down from the planes told us that we were containing some fires but that for every one we stopped two more were started by lightning striking trees in the dry forest. They'd never seen so many.

Eight days later we had finished all we could on our fire. It had nearly gone out. We were encamped on a ridge, looking out across the ruins of smoldering trees. Little fires were still burning here and there. It was too far to hike back to the base camp, so we settled in for the night.

The skies were clear. All was quiet. The silence was occasionally broken by nighthawks that flew high into the dark sky then shot straight down, opening their wings just before crashing into the ground, producing a booming sound that could be heard for miles. One came down almost on top of us, again and again, so close we felt we had to duck. We were probably camped close to his mate and her nest.

It was cold that night, despite my wool short coat. The ground where I was lying was damp—almost mud—from a recent rain. Coals left over from the forest fire were still glowing nearby, so I pulled some embers together, stoked them up with added wood, moved over to my newly built fire, curled up with my back against it, and went sound asleep, comfortably warmed.

I awoke with a start! The seat of my pants was burning! No time to take them off. I rolled over in the mud, rubbing my backside in the damp ground until the flames went out, then quickly pulled off my smoking pants to examine the damage. There was a large black hole in my Levis, my underpants were singed, and my skin was red. It hurt for days. My friends back in base camp told me to put butter on it.

After ten days the job was over. The truck took us in to the Anaconda Copper Co. office in Missoula where we were paid off in cash. Remembering previous advice, I ventured cautiously out into the street, looking both ways, money tucked away into an inside coat pocket. As I walked towards the post office, four rough-looking men began to follow me.

As fast as possible, I ran to the post office, slipped inside the door, went quickly up to a clerk, pulled the money out, and placed it on the counter. I kept ten dollars hidden away. The clerk made out a money order and gave me a stamped envelope which I addressed to my mother, jotted a short note to tell her I was doing fine and would be home soon, and deposited it directly into the Out-of-State letter slot.

The men stopped outside. They looked in through the window. I waited inside until they left, then cautiously glanced both ways and hurried up a side street, trying to find a boarding house where I could take a bath, clean up, and get a good night's sleep.

The next hour reminded me of Winnemucca. On each house there was a sign, "ROOMS TO RENT. VACANCY." I rang the doorbells. After one look at me, the response was always the same: "We have no rooms. Go away!"

Trying to think objectively about what I must have looked like, wearing a mud-crusted black short-coat, dirty face, unshaven, stringy hair, and backpack, I smiled to myself. But I also muttered epithets under my breath at the room keepers.

Then there was a breakthrough! A portly, almost pleasant lady looked down on me from the stairs above, head cocked sidewise.

"You don't look like the usual tramp."

"I'm a college boy."

"You're awfully dirty for a college boy! Worse than a lot of tramps I've seen. Got any money?"

I pulled out a silver dollar from my coat pocket.

"'You're awfully dirty for a college boy!' observed the landlady.
I filled the tub deeply with hot water, slipped into it, and soaked. How wonderful!"

"All right. Come around to the back door. I don't want anybody to see you coming into my house looking like *that*!"

I proceeded to the back door. She handed me a bathrobe and pointed to the porch bathroom that contained a long, white, deep tub.

"Hand me your dirty clothes. I'll wash them for you. Your room is the first one on the right."

I passed my clothes out to her, filled the tub deeply with hot water, slipped into it, and soaked. How wonderful! After the water gurgled down the spout, I cleaned the remaining dirt off the white tub and chuckled to myself over an old joke my sister Helen had told me: "Somebody left a ring in the bathtub. Was it yours?"

Then—into bed! White, clean, lightly starched sheets and a warm blanket! I slept from noon until eight o'clock the next morning. A bed never felt so good.

Going Home

I was ready to go home to my family and back to my college studies. I had made what seemed to me quite a lot of money, enough so I wouldn't have to work such long hours during my senior year. I gloated that I had spent almost none of it.

But—how to get home? Three choices: the bus cost too much, the traintops were not good to travel on alone, or hitchhiking. I started to wend my way to the highway outside of Missoula, clean and fresh-looking (I thought), more like a college boy than a tramp. Should be easy to catch rides.

Strolling along, humming to myself, I saw a flash of lightning followed by a sudden jolt of thunder not more than a second later. It must have been very close. Rain began to pour down. The passenger railway station was across the street, so I ducked under its corrugated metal awning for cover.

What happened next I'll never forget. There was a drinking fountain inside the station, so I decided to take a long drink of water before going out on the highway. Approaching the fountain, I noticed that its drinking head was round and white, made of porcelain, with the words "Haws, Berkeley" printed on it in black letters.

As I reached for the handle there was a loud crack of thunder that reverberated through the empty building. Instantly a bright, jagged line of fire rose six inches out of the fountainhead, waved around in the air, wriggling like a snake's tongue, then dropped back and disappeared. It was exactly where my face would have been a couple of seconds later.

I decided I didn't need any water. A bench was nearby, so I sat down, shaking. I had come frighteningly close to being electrocuted! (Somebody up there must have been watching over me.) Pulling myself together, I picked up my pack and walked out to the highway where I stood on the curb and raised my thumb, still trembling.

The first ride came quickly. The driver was a traveling salesman. He took me west and south through the Bitterroot Mountains and Nez Perce Indian country to Boise. There I slept behind a billboard on the south side of town. The short-coat saved me, again, from a cold summer night.

My direction from Boise was south across a corner of eastern Oregon and through the Nevada desert to Winnemucca. I sensed problems. How many cars would be traveling that lonely route? Would any of them be willing to pick up a stranger when it was a hundred miles between towns, and small towns at that? I'd have to find out. No turning back now.

Within fifteen minutes an old, rough-skinned, weather-beaten rancher wearing a broad-rimmed cowboy hat and driving a rattletrap Ford pickup truck pulled onto the gravel at the side of the road. I ran up to him to ask which way he was headed. He was going part way to Winnemucca, he said, maybe eighty miles, and would like some company.

"Going home to my ranch. Came up to Boise for grub and shopping. Get in!"

So I pulled open the squeaky door and got in. The ride was rough, but the company was pleasant. I learned more about Nevada desert ranches than I cared to know. What I remember best about that ride was where the rancher turned off the highway. We had traveled sixty or seventy miles through barren desert when he pointed off towards the left.

"Here's where I turn in," he announced.

I couldn't imagine where he meant. No road that I could see, no house, no anything. But then we came to it. There, crossing a barely visible dirt path, was a rickety wooden gate with a sliding bar and a padlocked chain to hold it closed. He pulled up, told me to get out, unlocked the gate, and swung it open.

"A few miles up the road there's a service station. Maybe you can get a ride from there."

Waving goodbye, he locked the gate behind him and started out across the desert. I watched his moving cloud of dust getting smaller and fainter off into the distance as far as I could see. The old Ford disappeared over a hill.

It was lonely on the highway. No cars passed. I walked in the desert heat, knapsack on my back, for several miles before I discerned far up ahead what looked like a service station. Why it should be there, I didn't know. No houses, no town, just a service station. Finally getting there, I was greeted by the young attendant. He was lonely, too. I asked about hitchhiking.

"If somebody stops for gas," he said, "it's all right to ask for a ride, but don't be pushy. We have a reputation to uphold here, you know. It's a long ninety miles to Winnemucca, and people don't like to pick up strangers out here."

Hour after hour I waited. One car roared past the station and whined up the highway without even slowing down. Several hours later a second car approached. I kept my fingers crossed, hoping it would stop. Then its brakes squealed and it turned in to the pump. Inside the vehicle were a man, a woman, and a child. While they were filling up,

Idaho

Hitchhiking in Idaho. "How many cars would be traveling that lonely route?"

I cautiously started talking to the man. I was a college boy, fought forest fires up in Missoula, was heading back to the University of California at Berkeley by way of Winnemucca. Was it possible . . . ?

It took a good deal of whispering, back and forth, between the man and his wife to finally, tentatively, say it might be all right if I rode along with them. After I climbed into the back seat with their five-year-old son and we started driving out across the desert, they still seemed uncomfortable. Gradually, after continued conversation, playing games with their little boy, and telling stories of my travels, they loosened up. The rest of the ninety-mile trip was relaxed, uneventful, and dull.

The way onward from Winnemucca to Reno and into California was easy. It took only two rides, the first to Reno and the second over the Donner Pass to Sacramento, where I called my mother to let her know that all was fine and that I'd be home soon. She was delighted and relieved, having last received my short, concerned note and the money order from Missoula.

Tired of hitchhiking and eager to get home, I squandered some of my new-earned wealth and took a Greyhound bus from Sacramento to Oakland for a dollar and a half and a local bus home for ten cents. Easier, I thought, than riding the rails. At least it was much more comfortable and more predictable.

Home

Mother was waiting for me at the door of our home near Mills College, where she had become director of student teachers. She threw her arms around me and hurried me inside so she could hear all the fascinating stories, even the one about the "bull" in Sparks. Dad, sister Helen, and brother Jim gathered around, too.

In the next few days Mother and I talked a lot about my adventures. She hadn't been worried about me, she said. Her philosophy was to see and learn about new things. She listened excitedly to my tales, glad that I could experience parts of the world she could never explore herself. There were risks in it but that's how you learn. When events were beyond your control, you had to "let go and let God."

I told her that sometimes, when you're out there all alone, looking up at myriads of stars, you think back to the base of strength that comes from home. I showed her the piece of paper, torn at the folds, that I carried with me all summer:

Merle B. Nordyke

The sap drains from the weed
And color from the sky
And man abroad has need
Of light to travel by—

Has need of speech to hear
In answer to his own
Of being warmed from fear
Of being less alone.

A man abroad will turn
And look, a way he knows,
Across the fields, to learn
If there a window glows.

A small and yellow square
With night on either hand
And he will hasten there
Across a darkening land—

That being, till he die,
Enough to travel by.
                                    David Morton

```
What a wonderful Mother you are!  The more I see of other
people the more I realize what a wonder you are - with such
flexibility, fullness, interest; welcoming new ideas, taking the
best of the new and holding to the best of the old, and discarding
the valueless of both.  If there's anything in the wide world I
can be thankful for, it's you - for your energy, your patience,
your humor and laughter, your understanding and backing, your
loving guidance.  I can't help but think that Mr. James wrote the
poem for you -

          All that you gave you have -
          That is the laborer's due.
          Wiser far than the best of us,
          This is the boon to the rest of us,
          Mellow Autumn - and you.
```

A note Bob wrote to his mother in 1939.

Dad's reaction to the trip was more pragmatic. He didn't like the idea of associating with bums. He had seen too many of them around the cattle yards in Woodland.

After a week with the family I crossed town to the boarding house in Berkeley to start my final year at Cal. Milton Lott was waiting to hear about my experiences and to exchange stories and ideas. The summer of '39 had been successful for both of us.

Epilogue: Philosophy for Life's Adventures

During the long summer, especially while droning along on the top of freight trains across the Nevada desert or gazing out across forested Montana mountains, I had plenty of time to think. What was I doing? Why was I out here, so far away from home? Why did I subject myself to cold, hunger, and repeated injustices when I could have been home, safe and comfortable?

One kind of answer came to me from the vivid memory of Professor Kurtz, a vibrant, portly, white haired, gentlemanly professor of English, with a neatly trimmed mustache. In class one day he was discussing the Bhagavad Gita. The great things in life, he said, all came together for him when he sped around the curves of a mountain road in his open-top Porsche, one arm in the air, exulting (though no one was listening), "What the hell!" A freedom, self-confidence, independence, belief in yourself, and indescribable inner glee that comes from being out there on your own, beholden to no one, responsible only to yourself. A feeling that wasn't attainable, I thought, if you're continuously surrounded by protective comforts.

An opposing answer kept cropping up in my mind, though. Suppose you're out there forever searching for something that is all the time at home, where you left it? What a loss that would be! I remembered the haunting lines in Melville's *Moby-Dick:*

Round the world! There is much in that sound to inspire proud feelings; but whereto does all that circumnavigation conduct? Only through numberless perils to the very point whence we started, where those we left behind secure were all the time before us.

T.S. Eliot said it another way: that the end of all our exploring will be to arrive where we started, and to know the place for the first time.

Even so, each time you come back from out there you're enriched by new ideas, unexpected intrusions, life-long friends, shaken prejudices, and memories that linger on forever. It forces growth.

As I thought back on it, the overriding value of the summer was the time I had by myself—to begin to gather together what I believed, to learn who I was. At nineteen, chock full of unformed idealism and swarming impressions, a young fellow needed time to pull his thoughts together.

Men journey to find themselves, James Michener once said. Money, position, fame are all of little consequence. But if a man knows the positions from which he will no longer retreat, the depth of his feeling for beauty, his honest goals—then he has found a mansion that he can inhabit for the rest of his life. I had time to think about that.

Roots. Self-confidence. Liberation. Excitement about the future. These were what the summer of '39 was all about.

Bob after an adventurous summer

Chapter Six

ᎶᏩ GALAPAGOS: RADIO OPERATOR ᎶᏩ

Radio School

The time was 1941. The Western World was in conflagration. Hitler had blitzed into Poland, the Baltics, Czechoslovakia, and now France. America, responding to the urging of Churchill and Roosevelt, was awakening to the need to stop the rolling German armies from consolidating continental Europe, overcoming England, and ruling the world.

My concerns were on a smaller scale. In May of 1940, at the age of 20, I had graduated from Berkeley, combining English Literature, Political Science, and Public Speaking, none of which prepared me for anything practical. Uncle Sam was hotly breathing down my neck, making it impossible to develop long-term plans. Along with myriads of other able-bodied young men, I signed up with my draft board and was given a number. It was anybody's guess when that number would come up, wafting me into combat as a foot soldier in front line trenches. That was disquieting.

One lazy, sultry afternoon while scanning the San Jose Mercury-Herald for jobs and schooling possibilities, I chanced on an ad for training in radio repair combined with radiotelegraph licensing. In two months, they said, they could prepare you for your ham and commercial radio licenses and, at the same time, for a job as a radio operator on ships at sea. Two birds with one stone! It would be fun to learn something new and maybe pick up a practical trade experience the Armed Forces could use—better than slogging through muddy trenches.

I hopped on a bus to San Francisco to sign up for the course. By the end of two months I felt comfortable repairing radio receivers and transmitters and was able to send and receive Morse code thirty words a minute. Not great, but enough to pass the commercial operator's license examination that only required twenty.

The time on the train up and back to San Francisco was spent studying . . . except for the persistence of a girl who kept bothering me. She climbed on the train after I did, often accompanied by a girl companion. They tended to settle down directly across the aisle from me. She was slim and neat, with marble skin, a long white neck, and blonde hair that billowed across her shoulders when she laughed. I had trouble keeping my attention on the books when she was there, and daydreamed about talking to her and maybe even touching her. I never got up enough nerve.

Radio Telegraph Operator License

With the commercial radiotelegraph license in hand, the teachers said my best chance for a job was on large tuna fishing boats which, by law, required a radio operator. The best place for that was in San Diego where the tuna fleet set out to Mexico, Central America, Panama, and the Galapagos Islands. No guarantee of a job, but it was worth a try.

Hitchhiking to San Diego

Early one morning, after cramming a backpack full of living necessities and waving good-bye to my family at our home in the Willow Glen suburb of San Jose, I hopped on a bus, got off at the main highway leading out of town, and started to hitchhike to San Diego.

The first ride was easy, to King City. The second was from a kind, pleasant, and talk-ative young African American who took me all the way to Los Angeles in a jalopy that rattled steadily along at forty miles an hour to Paso Robles and then across the hills into the sweltering San Joaquin Valley, with only one stop for lunch at Bakersfield. We ordered hamburgers together. He explained how good it was to be able to eat with a white man in California.

"If we was in eastern Texas," he told me, "I'd have to go to my side of the restaurant and you to yours. Couldn't sit together. There'd be separate toilets and drinking fountains, too."

That was hard for me to understand.

He dropped me off on the coast road at Santa Monica.

By this time it was getting late in the afternoon. Hotels cost too much. Might as well push on. So back on the road, sticking my thumb up in the air for another ride. After an hour of steady discouragement, a new, sleek, red Chrysler convertible with the top down slid to a stop and waved me in. The driver was a well-dressed man with a trimmed moustache, thin, a little effeminate.

"Where you going?" he called.

"To San Diego for a job on a tuna fishing boat."

"I'm going the same way. I'll take you all the way there."

"Great!"

Off we went through Santa Ana and into San Clemente, near the ocean. The cold fog moved in "on little cats' feet" as Carl Sandberg's poem said. The man stopped the car and I helped him put the roof up.

As we approached Oceanside, he said, "It's getting late. Why don't we stay over at a motel? I'll pay for it." I could feel his hand touch my leg.

"I'd rather not."

At the next stop sign I opened the door, jumped out, collected my pack from the back seat, thanked him for the ride, and quickly walked away.

I started looking for a place to stay for the night. The Oceanside Shell Service Station, a block down the street, showed yellow lights burning through the fog. Approaching, I could see the indistinct form of a man inside, sitting at a desk in front of a cash register, closing up for the night. A bright red electric heater was aimed at his feet. I tapped on the window. He slid it open a few inches and gruffly asked what I wanted.

"Hi! I'm a college boy trying to get to San Diego for a job. Is there a chance I might sleep on the floor in your room, or in the garage? It's awfully cold out here."

We talked a bit. He asked how I got this far, why I hadn't taken the bus, what kind of a job it was. Gradually he became more cordial.

"The boss wouldn't want me to let you stay in here or even inside the garage. He's afraid of being robbed. Maybe you can sleep behind the building. At least there's less wind there."

Fair enough. I thanked him and went behind the station, pulled a tarp off a pile of wood to protect me from the wind and from the persistent damp fog, and went sound asleep.

Early next morning the fog was gone, the sun was out, and the air was soft and warm. The first car slid to a stop and took me all the way to San Diego.

The Union

Word was that no job as a radio operator was possible without joining the union, and it was hard to get into the union without a lot of experience. That seemed to leave me out. Had to try, anyway. So I signed up for a room at the YMCA, left my pack, and walked to the waterfront where there was a small run-down shack with a sign, "International Telecommunications Union."

Inside was a heavy-set, round-faced, bearded, affable Portuguese man who called himself Joe. He explained that there was very little chance of a radio operator job opening on the tuna fleet, but once in a while one appears out of nowhere. "Sign up and leave your phone number. Don't call us; we'll call you," he said.

Next morning I was awakened by an almost frantic call from Joe. He told me that a big tuna boat, the M.V. *Madeirense*, was set to sail this afternoon for Costa Rica and the Galapagos Islands and would be back in thirty to sixty days. Their "sparks" (the name for all radiotelegraph operators) had left the ship in a huff and they needed a replacement—right now!

"Can you be ready by three o'clock?"

"Of course! Sounds great!" I was jumping with excitement.

"Do you think you can handle the job?"

"Of course!" The response masked my hidden concerns.

"Stop by here and pay your union dues, then go down to the boat."

There was a small administrative problem, though: I wasn't supposed to leave the U.S. without notifying my draft board in advance. Maybe I could do that by telegram once I got out to sea, en route to Costa Rica?

So I signed out of the Y., threw all my belongings over my shoulder, and walked (almost ran) to the union building, then to the dock.

The M.V. Madeirense

How beautiful she was! White, sleek, clean, bigger than I had imagined. I walked tentatively up the gangplank of the M.V. *Madeirense*, looking for the captain.

The captain was still busy on shore, but John, his tall, lean, and friendly nephew, showed me about the boat. He was full of information. This was a Portuguese tuna boat, one of the larger ones. It cost $250,000 to build, and was only three years old. It stretched one hundred forty-nine feet from bow to stern and it was designed to be just one foot less than the length required by law for a medical officer and assistant engineer to be hired for

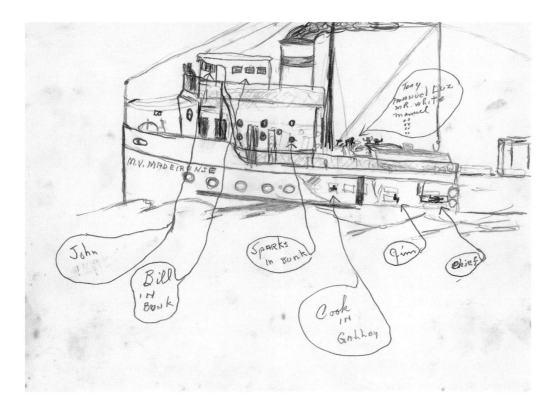

The M.V. Madeirense

every trip. Its capacity was two hundred tons of tuna, frozen and stored below deck in the holds—less than the three hundred tons of its sister ship, the Azoreana, docked next to us.

The ship was owned by a group of relatives who put up an equal amount of money. They came from the Madeira Islands off Portugal, where their forebears were fishermen, too. All the crew were relatives except for the chief engineer. Before each trip the owners elected a captain. If the catch was especially good and the boat returned to port with a full load of fish within thirty to forty-five days, he was usually re-elected. If the catch was poor or the time getting home to their lonely and concerned families was delayed, there was a meeting with all the owners. The captain was first vilified in front of everybody—often with fists shaking in the air—and then voted out.

Only three of the twelve crew aboard spoke fluent English: my guide John, Frank the chief engineer, and I. Henry Gonzalves, the navigator, could get his ideas across in broken English, but he reverted to Portuguese when he was mad. Antonio Francisco, this trip's captain, could hardly speak English at all. The others, John said, would be cordial but wouldn't communicate much.

John showed me my cabin. It was on the port side amidships and was larger than any except the captain's, but pretty small. On one side was a wide bench with a radio receiver and transmitter on top and two motor-generators on the floor beneath—a large one for the transmitter, a tiny one for the receiver. It was a powerful set, John told me, 250 watts, with no capability for voice transmission, only CW (continuous wave) requiring Morse code. You could communicate anywhere in the world with that. A well-worn brass semi-automatic key was firmly attached to the bench next to the transmitter. I wondered if my thirty words a minute would be enough to receive and transmit whatever the captain wanted to communicate. The rotating chair in front of the bench was clamped to the floor to keep rough seas from throwing it around. My bunk, washbasin, and toilet were on the opposite side of the cabin. There wasn't space for anything else. I dropped my backpack and coat on the bunk.

Then John carried on the tour. He pointed out the metal grating that stuck three feet out from the boat's hull all around the stern and half way up both sides. The fishermen would jump onto this when the chummer gave the shout that fish were biting. Tuna were caught with barbless hooks at the end of short lines. Small ones, weighing 100–150 pounds, were called "one-pole" fish—one fisherman, one pole, one line, one hook. Middle sized ones (150–250 pounds) were "two-pole" fish, and large ones (250–350 pounds) were "three-pole" fish: three men, each with a pole, and three lines tied to a single hook. As soon as fishing started, the men would stand on the grating in their rubber clothes, waist-high in water some of the time, completely out of water at other times as the huge swells alternately raised the boat in the air and plunged it deep in the water. A

Radio officers' frank to transmit wireless messages. "I wondered if my thirty words a minute would be enough to receive and transmit whatever the captain wanted."

No. 1232   1941

RADIO OFFICERS' FRANK
GLÓBE WIRELESS LTD.
MESSAGES SENT BY

MR. ROBERT A. NORDYKE
OF A PERSONAL SOCIAL CHARACTER

will be transmitted between all points of the GLOBE WIRELESS SYSTEM or by any GLOBE WIRELESS coastal station or will be accepted from ship radio stations by GLOBE coastal radio stations free of all tolls that would regularly accrue to the Company in a total amount not in excess of $50.00 for the calendar year of 1941.

THIS FRANK EXPIRES
DECEMBER 31, 1941

EXECUTIVE VICE PRESIDENT

Subject to the conditions on the reverse hereof.

F.C.C. FORM NO. 735

Photograph is required

**QUESTIONNAIRE FOR COMMERCIAL AND
AMATEUR RADIO OPERATORS**

1. NAME _Nordyke_ _Robert_ _Allan_
             Surname   First   Middle

No   2½"
                    in size

2. _821 Plaza Drive, San Jose, Calif._
            Your present home address

3. _July 14, 1919_   _Woodland, Calif., U.S.A. (Yolo Co.)_
       Date of birth   Your place of birth (city or town, county, state, country)

Questionnaire and photo for commercial and amateur radio operators.

low railing kept the men from being dragged overboard when big tuna struck their lines, and it kept sharks, attracted by blood, from getting too close.

In the middle of the central deck John jerked open some wooden lids to let me peer down into the dark, empty, smelly, refrigerated holds where the tuna would be frozen soon after they were caught. The smell was overwhelming. One of the holds was to be half filled with warm ocean water in Costa Rica to store live bait fish we'd net in the Gulf of Nicoya for "chumming"—throwing them over the side to attract tuna.

Along the starboard walkway, directly opposite my cabin, a small Catholic prayer room was pungent with fresh flowers, renewed by the wives before leaving port. When heavy seas and frightening storms required prayers, the crew would line up for their turn in the chapel.

Up the stairs above the main deck curved the captain's bridge. The spokes of the huge varnished steering wheel radiated out in a circle next to the navigator's maps, compass, chronometer, and sextant. Overhead, atop the mainmast, towered the crow's nest; steel spikes stuck out from both sides of the mast to help the men clamber to the top for visual observation of circling birds and finely rippling water that evidenced schools of tuna. My radio antenna wire sagged between the fore and aft masts.

Out to Sea

Gangplank clanked, whistle moaned, crew waved, girls threw kisses, and the ship creaked slowly out from the dock. Excitement filled the air, but tears overflowed too as the men and their wives, girlfriends, and families waved goodbye, not to be together again for several months.

"Be sure to send us a telegram when you start for home. We'll be ready for you!" they called out from the shore.

"Of course we will. Always do!" the men shouted back.

The harbor receded. So did Point Loma where the well-to-do Portuguese fishermen established their homes. John pointed out his impressive house as we passed. Then, from thirty miles out to sea, we followed the coast of Baja California towards the south. Seagulls soared, fluttered, and dived behind us. The rumbling rhythm of the motor, the deep blue of the ocean off the bow, and the rolling white water off the stern were exhilarating. What a feeling of freedom and adventure!

Freedom. Oh, my gosh! I'd better send a telegram to my draft board to let them know I've left the country without their approval. How do I phrase that? Can't turn back now! Better rev up the transmitter and send them a telegram.

In the radio room I flipped on the motor-generators, the receiver, and the transmitter, and waited. I'd never seen such big and impressive equipment before. There were lots of dials—probably works like the smaller ones I learned on, though.

Something began to smell. Awful. Then it smoked. A funny noise came from under the bench—the transmitter's motor-generator! Quick—shut it off! The sound went away and the smoke cleared, gradually. It still smelled bad. Try again. Bad noise. Smell. Smoke. Turn it off!

Frank

That's when I first got acquainted with Frank, the chief engineer. John had told me that Frank knew everything mechanical and electrical about this boat and if I ever had any trouble, call him. He came up on the ladder from below, responding to my concerned call, chewing on \an unlit cigar, engineer's striped cap tilted over his bushy brows to shield the bright sun, overalls greasy, clean-shaven face spattered with oil from the diesel engines.

I told him my trouble. He smiled weakly, as if he knew something I didn't know.

"Well, let's get on with it." His approach was no-nonsense.

Frank turned out to be my savior. First he worked on the motor-generator with me. It had been shorted out, he said, by one of the crew and maybe damaged by the sparks who left the boat in a huff after the last trip.

By manipulations that only Frank could explain, he fixed up the generator so it would last three or four minutes before it got hot.

"When you transmit, you've got to be ready and work fast. Send anything you need to send quickly, then shut it off. The receiver has its own generator. It's OK, so you can get time ticks for the navigator," Frank explained.

Telegram to the draft board.

Mackay Radio

Postal   Telegraph

CHARGE ACCOUNT NUMBER

CASH NO.	TOLLS

CHECK

TIME FILED   (STANDARD TIME)

DCC 8

Send the following message "VIA MACKAY RADIO," subject to the rules, regulations and rates of Mackay Radio and Telegraph Company set forth in its tariffs and on file with regulatory authorities.

DOMESTIC SERVICES } 15 WORDS FOR THE USUAL PRICE OF 10

NR 1 CK 19   MV MADEIRENSE   0450 GMT 15

DRAFT BOARD 110
SANJOSE (CALIF)

AT SEA AS RADIO OPERATOR BACK TWO MONTHS NO TIME

TO GET PERMIT SORRY

NORDYKE

OFFICE OR ANY POSTAL TELEGRAPH OFFICE.

ANCISCO......GARFIELD 1303	SEATTLE ....ELLIOT 4212
D .... TEMPLEBAR 3360	TACOMA ....MAIN 6101
IGELES ......TRINITY 0731	PORTLAND ....ATWATER 6484
EGO.................MAIN 4177	NEW ORLEANS......RAYMOND 9237

H OR RING POSTAL CALL BOX.

August 19, 1941.
(Date)

PERMIT OF LOCAL BOARD FOR REGISTRANT TO DEPART FROM THE UNITED STATES

This is to certify that ___Robert___ ___Allan___ ___Nordyke___
(First name)   (Middle name)   (Last name)

Order No. __2847__, Serial No. __517__, Class _____, Division _____
(Number)   (Letter)

a registrant of this Local Board has applied for a permit to depart from the United States, and this Local Board, being convinced that said registrant is not likely to be called for military service during the proposed absence and that the granting of such permit will not result in the evasion of or interference with the execution of the Selective Service Law, hereby authorizes the said registrant to depart from the United States and to remain absent therefrom for __(90) Ninety days__
(Designate period of absence)

In his application the registrant gave this information:

1. Countries to be visited __Central America__

2. Individuals or organizations represented __Van Camp Sea Food Co.__

3. Nature of business __Radio Operator   Fisherman__

Description of registrant:

RACE		HEIGHT (Approx.)		WEIGHT (Approx.)		COMPLEXION	
White	xx	5'11"		155		Sallow	
		EYES		HAIR		Light	xx
Negro		Blue		Blonde		Ruddy	
		Gray		Red		Dark	
Oriental		Hazel	xx	Brown	xx	Freckled	
		Brown		Black		Light brown	
Indian		Black		Gray		Dark brown	
				Bald		Black	
Filipino							

Other obvious physical characteristics that will aid in identification _____

Date of birth __July 14, 1919__

M J Enos
Member of Local Board.

NOTICE TO DECLARANT ALIENS (ALIENS WITH "FIRST PAPERS").—Before leaving the country, get a re-entry permit at the nearest office of the Federal Immigration and Naturalization Service.
D. S. S. Form 351   U. S. GOVERNMENT PRINTING OFFICE   16—17327

Permit from draft board to depart from the United States.

Frank, the chief engineer.

What's Sparks For?

If the transmitter could only work a few minutes at a time, I wondered why I was needed. Frank set me straight. "First, a ship of our size has to have a licensed radio operator, by rule of the feds, no matter what. The captain has to have you here, so relax. You'll get paid," Frank said.

From the crew's point of view, they need you to send a telegram home a few days before we arrive back in San Diego, so their families and girl friends will be at the dock when they return after six or eight weeks of separation. At the same time, you've got to notify Van Camp to put the public health doctor on standby when you come into port; otherwise the crew can't get off the boat to greet their waiting families for hours, maybe even overnight. You'd better be able to send those telegrams, or it's your hide! I saw that happen once, he warned. It was grim!

I was getting concerned. What else?

Well, Frank continued, weather reports are occasionally useful to the captain, especially if a storm is headed our way, but once we pass "Tepec", reports aren't usually needed. Tepec, I learned, is the Isthmus of Tehuantepec, the slim waist of Central America. Strong, gusty northwesterly winds funnel from the Gulf of Mexico across the narrow isthmus and far out the other side into the Pacific Ocean, producing a band of choppy sea a hundred miles wide ("You can feel the whipping wind and bumping waves against the port side the minute you enter it. When you get to the far edge, you'll sail smoothly out the other side, like glass."). Once we pass Tepec, nobody cares about the weather, especially out around Galapagos where the U.S. Navy has never seen a storm, or even rain, since it started keeping records in 1884.

Sparks is good for another thing, he continued. Each trip out the captain sets up a list of secret codes so he can let his good relatives on other boats (the ones he's getting along with this season) know how good or bad the fishing is. There may be days or weeks of catching nothing; then you try to find out if somebody is catching a lot of tuna someplace else so you can go there, even if it's hundreds of miles away in Panama or Costa Rica or Galapagos.

On the other hand, when you're loading up with twenty or thirty tons of tuna a day, you want to tell the good guys to come on over to join in the catch, and tell the bad guys you're not catching anything at all. Keeps them away. John will give you the code list for this trip. It's kept secret till we're out to sea.

"Oh, I almost forgot," Frank added, "the most important reason for your being here, I can tell you for sure, is to give the navigator his time tick every day. As you know, the navigator's position will be off by one mile for every four seconds his clock is wrong." (I didn't know.) "That can be dangerous. So he'll want you to give him the right time, to the second, twice a day. I'm sure you learned all about that in radio school." (I hadn't even heard of it.)

I thanked Frank for the information. Secretly it made me queasy in the stomach. Why didn't they teach me these things in the school? What if I couldn't get the transmitter going long enough to send the telegrams to the families and girl friends? What if I couldn't warn the captain of a storm coming up this side of Tepec? What if I couldn't find out where the good fishing was? What if I couldn't tell the navigator the exact time?

Time Ticks

"Sparks! Come up here! Got to know time!" It was Henry, the navigator, calling from the bridge.

"Coming!" I said with as much confidence as I could muster.

Up the ladder Captain Francisco was turning the wheel with one hand, scanning ahead through his binoculars in the other, glancing at the compass. He nodded to me as I opened the door. Henry was poring over his maps, drawing lines, and looking at his chronometer. "Got to know time! I take clock to your cabin, you tell me time."

"I'm busy right now," I said. "You come down a little later, OK?"

I figured that would give me a chance to find out what a time tick was, how to get it, what it meant, and how to interpret it to Henry.

Emergency call to Frank; he knows everything. Frank told me he didn't know much but he could give me a general idea. He tried to explain. First, you carefully tune your receiver to the Naval station in Washington, D.C.

"I think it's NPG, but I don't know where it is on the dial. When you hear it, you'll know it. In Morse they repeatedly announce who they are and on what frequencies they're broadcasting. A few minutes before each quarter-hour they start sending little dits and then they send a long tone, lasting about a minute. When that stops (or maybe when it starts), it's exactly on the quarter hour. If you hear that, call Henry. He knows better than I do what it sounds like." Frank disappeared down the dark steep ladder into the engine room. Nothing was found about time ticks in any book I had, so Frank's explanation was all there was.

That started the most intense, frustrating, anxious, fatiguing twelve hours in my life. Sitting in front of the short-wave receiver and wearing headphones, I began at the lower end of the thirty-six meter band and worked slowly towards the top. There were dozens of stations, barely separated from each other. Every station had to be listened to long enough to discover its call letters, to determine if there were any sounds like Frank described, to listen most closely for NPG (-. .--. --.).

I *had* to get the exact time. I couldn't let the navigator down. He might hit an island. It would be my fault. Why didn't they teach me this in radio school? What will the captain say? What does a time tick sound like?

As I moved from one station to the next, each had different high-pitched sounds, reverberating in my ears. They all began to fuse into each other. I couldn't eat, couldn't drink, and cold sweat dripped off my forehead as my hands moved the round black dial painfully from one station to the next to the next, listening, listening, listening. I thought I'd go out of my mind.

At two in the afternoon and again at six I thought I had the station. I ran up to the navigator on the bridge. "I've got it!" He came down the ladder to my radio shack and listened. "Not it. Sounds like it, not it. I know it when I hear. Got to get it for me—soon!" and he shuffled off. Each time was a severe letdown.

Back to the table, on and on, one station to the next.

Then it happened. It was eight o'clock at night, after twelve hours of intense, grueling pressure. There it was, clear and loud: "NPG, NPG, NPG, dit dit dit, dit dit dit, NPG."

I raced up to the navigator. "I got it! Really have!" He brought his chronometer down and we listened together. "NPG, NPG, dit dit dit."

"That's it! That's it! Now wait for the long one. It'll stop at exactly eight. You'll see!"

And it did. In all my life I had never heard such a beautiful sound. He corrected his chronometer (it was off by ten seconds), thanked me, and went back to the bridge.

I dropped on my bunk without taking off my clothes, and fell heavily asleep. Next thing I knew, John was shaking my shoulder.

"Time to get up! You've slept all night and all day. You sick? Dinner's ready."

Tepec

The *Madeirense* plowed steadily southward, fifty miles off Baja California, past Cape San Lucas, then hugged the coast of Mexico, passing the twinkling lights of Mazatlán and Manzanillo and Acapulco in the distance. A trailing thermometer told us the ocean temperature had risen from seventy-six degrees at San Diego to nearly ninety degrees. We were headed to Puntarenas, Costa Rica. There we would fill one of the holds with bait fish before taking off to the Galapagos Islands.

Then it hit. The wind came up and the waves slapped the port side of the boat repeatedly, bumping me around in my chair, making it nearly impossible to read or write. Without previous warning it would have been frightening. But here it was, as Frank predicted—Tepec. The whipping winds sent spray across our bow; the great rising swells rose above us; the rough white chops superimposed themselves on top of the swells. Now I knew what they meant by Tepec. For a full twenty-four hours this continued, unabated.

Almost as suddenly as it started, the slapping waves faded away, the winds died down, and the sea turned calm and glassy, leaving me with a deep feeling of peace. I spent hours forward at the bow leaning against the rail, gazing down on the sharp prow slicing through the turquoise sea, peeling away the pellucid water on both sides. That day I wrote a note to my sister Betty: "Have you ever known the bright blue water of the ocean to draw up inside you and make you laugh?"

On we plowed, down the coast past Guatemala, El Salvador, Honduras, and northern Costa Rica, turning into the Gulf of Nicoya at Cape Blanco, chugging to a stop a few hundred yards off the Puntarenas dock. Anchor splashed, chain rumbled, motor cut, landing skiffs lowered, crew scrambled precariously down the rope ladder, outboard motor string pulled, and off we went in a puff of smoke to visit the port town where we planned to stay for two days while netting bait fish in the shallow gulf.

Puntarenas

The day was hot and muggy as we strolled into town from the dock. Low-lying wooden buildings in disrepair lined the main road. Unpaved streets were soaked from continuing rains, forcing everyone onto the wooden sidewalks, under tattered awnings, or into the ubiquitous beer parlors. Brown-skinned men, women, and children wearing bright colored clothes gave us friendly nods as we passed. They often stepped aside and stared, seeming curious, since the only foreign visitors were occasional fishermen stopping by for bait. Outdoor fruit stands overflowed with pineapples, bananas, and melons. Little storefronts displayed trays of belts, purses and shoes—high quality, they said, made from alligators they caught in the jungle swamps outside the town beyond the last house.

Darkness settled in. Scattered clouds faded into the moonless night. I ventured out into the village to see how the people lived. The streets were narrow and unpaved, lined with hundreds of little box houses, row on row, each lighted and each with a radio playing the same loud music. Sheet lightning lit up the entire sky in flashes, one after the other, bright enough to read by, each flash accompanied by a chorus of squawks from the radios.

Maria

Wandering back to the town's center I spotted John and Frank in an open-air beer parlor, surrounded by brightly dressed young ladies. One sat on John's knee.

"Have a beer. Which one do you want?" John asked.

I understood the first part of his statement, but was unsure of the second. Before I had time to think about it, a young girl pulled up a chair next to mine, put her arm on my shoulder, and whispered in my ear, "Me Maria."

She was pretty, I thought. Long black hair tied behind with a red ribbon, sparkling brown eyes, light brown skin, yellow dress that hung off both shoulders. It was fascinating and confusing to a 21-year-old boy a thousand miles from home.

A little later I had to go to the men's room. I proceeded to relieve myself into an open metal trough. In the process someone touched my arm. It was Maria, standing next to me.

"You come with Maria!" she said, pulling on my sleeve. I was startled. Her voice sounded authoritative.

It was her perfume and availability versus my home, church, and YMCA teachings. I made my decision, then, and darted down the covered sidewalk to the dock, onto the waiting skiff, and back to the *Madeirense.*

On the way a sudden downpour cooled me off.

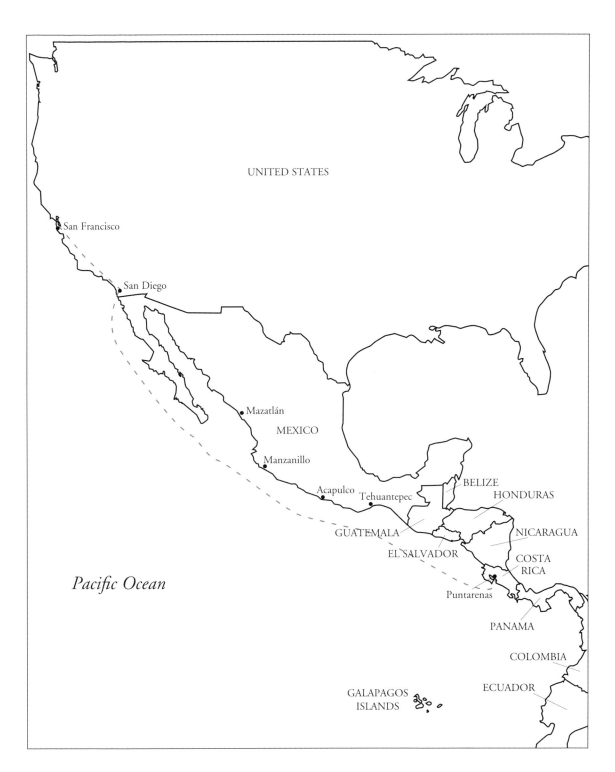

The trip south

Three-pole fishing

Chapter Seven

❧ GALAPAGOS: FISHING ❧

Out to the Islands

By next afternoon we had filled a sloshing tank with baitfish and started off towards the Galapagos Islands. These volcanic islands triangulate six hundred miles southwest of Costa Rica and six hundred miles straight out into the Pacific from Ecuador, the little country that sits on the bulge of South America on the equator. The Humboldt Current, migrating north from the Antarctic along the coast of Chile, brings coolness with it. At Ecuador it turns abruptly westward into the Pacific, bathing the islands with myriads of forms of sea and land life, even penguins.

Our trailing thermometer at Puntarenas had indicated ninety-three degrees. Gradually it fell to ninety, eighty, seventy, and finally sixty-five degrees as we entered the Humboldt Current and approached the islands.

The trip to our fishing grounds took almost two days. Odd jobs were finished off, fishing gear repaired, poles separated into one-, two-, and three-pole packets so they could be snapped up quickly without confusion at the first sighting of tuna. The air cooled and conversation slacked off. At last I could enjoy time to read Joseph Conrad's intense and unforgettable *Lord Jim* that had been hidden at the bottom of my knapsack.

There was also time to peruse an old U.S. Navy booklet that was left on my desk by some previous radio operator. Short descriptions of the Pacific Ocean in this region, and the Galapagos Islands were included.

Look Who Came to Dinner!

Towards evening of the second day out of Costa Rica we sighted Culpepper Island (now called Darwin). It was small, only a few acres, with a high arch in the middle that let you see through, all the way to islands beyond. Captain Francisco decided to bypass Culpepper; there wouldn't be many tuna around it, he guessed. Isabella was just ahead—probably better fishing. We'd drop anchor there and reconsider in the morning.

The night was dark and moonless. Our ship cast a halo of bright light all around us, extending out a hundred feet before abruptly fusing into black. I stood on the main deck, just above the rising and falling swells, leaning over the railing to watch a commotion that was starting to roil up the smooth ocean surface below. Little diaphanous flying fish skittered in all directions, an occasional one landing on our deck (they were a treat to eat, John said, almost as good as Wahoo). Why were there so many? Attracted by the lights, I supposed. Why were they flitting around so nervously?

The answer to that came quickly. As I watched, dozens of dark shadowy forms, five to ten feet long, moved into the light from out of the darkness, fins cutting the surface with hardly a ripple, undulating ever so slowly towards stationary, quivering flying fish. A sudden rush of turbulent water sent a fish off in the air, or (unfortunately for the fish) it was too late, and the shark had its meal.

I counted over 60 sharks within the ship's light swath and, just for fun, poked two of them with the end of a fish gaff. I decided not to go snorkeling that night.

Searching for Tuna

Next morning we pulled up anchor and moved slowly towards Santa Maria Island, eyes out for signs of tuna. The skipper of the *Azoreana*, one of our captain's cousins, had radioed a coded message that fishing was good there and invited us over. Half a day later our spotter, sitting in the crow's nest on the mainmast, let out a shout and pointed to circling birds and ruffled surface water off the starboard bow. All fishermen rushed to their appointed positions, tentatively awaiting further instructions.

We plowed slowly forward towards the moving center of the activity. Manuel Blanco was the official chummer. He rushed to the port deck and began throwing live bait overboard from a bucket to attract tuna, estimate their size, decide the number of poles needed (nearly all tuna in a school are the same size), and whether they would or wouldn't bite. No matter how many fish you saw, if they won't bite you might as well leave for someplace else.

As we approached, I saw the most amazing sight. Big yellow-fin tuna were lined up in the same direction by the hundreds, motionless in the crystal water all around the ship. Layer on layer they extended downwards and outwards as far as eye could see.

But they weren't biting. The little fish that Manuel threw out just wiggled off through the maze of uninterested tuna.

Manuel stopped chumming. The captain wanted him to keep trying. He wouldn't. That made the captain angry.

"Meester White!" he yelled (he called Manuel Blanco that when he was mad). "Chum!" Manuel didn't move.

"Meester Francisco," Manuel replied without looking at the captain. "Don' tell me chum!" (The chummer was a professional. He knew when to chum).

The captain started towards Mr. White, fist raised. Mr. White turned towards the captain, fist shaking in the air. Both were livid. Peering out from behind my cabin door, only a few yards away, I felt murderous tension in the air.

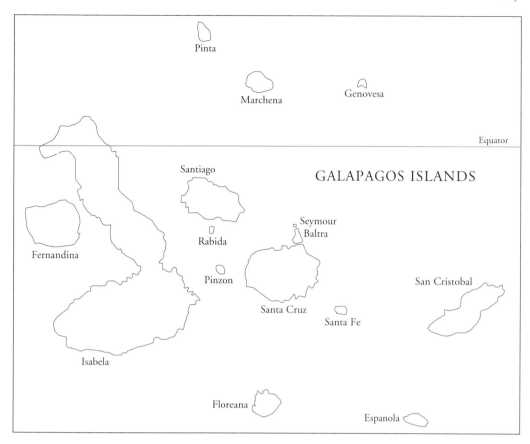

As they approached closer, face to face, fists still shaking and both still shouting, the anger suddenly died. Fists dropped. Both turned around and sulked off in opposite directions. The captain quietly ascended the ladder to his wheelhouse, revved up the engine, and took off to Santa Maria.

That day I learned something about chumming, tuna, and the Portuguese.

Elmer

Black and white penguins, about two feet high, swam near shore. Except for their small size, they looked like any self-respecting penguin should. In earlier times they must have been swept along by the Humboldt Current and floated from the Antarctic to the equator.

One of the fishermen caught a little penguin and brought it aboard the *Madeirense*. We called him (or her) Elmer. I tried to feed him but he was defensive, wouldn't eat, and wouldn't be tamed, so I guided him to the edge of the deck and urged him overboard. He dived into the water with hardly a splash and undulated rapidly off in the distance, towards shore.

Elmer, the little penguin,
aboard the Madeirense.

Now and then we spotted a school of killer whales. They leaped in and out of the water gracefully and simultaneously, like a team of oversized dolphins in training. John told me that if you were catching tons of tuna and a school of these whales came along, the tuna would take a deep dive and not come up for days. You might as well move on to new fishing grounds.

The Azoreana

We dropped anchor off Santa Maria to await daybreak and try to get reliable fishing information from our captain's cousin, the master of the *Azoreana* that was anchored a quarter mile off our port bow. The moon was a golden crescent, casting a faintly glimmering pathway across the smooth waters, fading between the long, quiet swells.

Frank suggested that he and I take the dinghy and row across to the *Azoreana* to see if they had tools to repair my transmitter's motor-generator. With the captain's permission (he thought we could obtain news about successful fishing without directly asking), John helped us drop the dinghy off the stern. We precariously found our footing in the wobbly little boat, carefully balancing to keep it from tipping over.

The dinghy was eight feet long, three feet wide, and had one set of oars. Frank took the oars and I settled back comfortably as we pushed off, crossed beyond our ship's lights, and rowed into the darkness towards the *Azoreana*. The stars were brilliant, the crescent moon curved low in the sky, and the night was completely quiet except for the rhythmic clinking of the oarlocks and the gentle touching of the oars to the water. I remembered the words in Knut Hamsun's *Growth of the Soil*, a novel of the Norwegian back country so beautiful it won him the Nobel Prize in literature: "He taught them about the moon, how when you can grip in the hollow side with your left hand it is waxing, and grip in with the right, it's on the wane. Remember that, boys!" I could grip it in my left hand; it would be larger tomorrow night.

My musing was brought up short by a shadow in the water next to the dinghy: a long, dark, barely perceptible form appeared off to one side, triangular fin cleaving the surface with hardly a ripple, moving along, silently accompanying, neither faster nor slower, just alongside, confident. Then there was another, only bigger, on the other side. It nudged the dinghy, giving it a little bump. What if it hit harder? What if it tipped us over?

Frank calmed me. "Don't worry. I don't think these fellows mean to hurt us. Just curious. They'll go away."

But they didn't go away. A third one, about twelve feet long, came next to us, close enough to touch. This one, especially, made me feel more uncomfortable. It swished away when an oar accidentally touched its body, only to return, closer. What if it snapped at an oar and pulled us over before we could release the oarlock?

The *Azoreana* wasn't far away now, but the distance was closing too slowly. The current seemed to be against us. Frank was tiring. He asked if I wanted to row.

"Not now!" I urged, trying not to sound uncooperative. "Not if we have to change positions! Too tippy!" He agreed.

At long last we pulled up beside the *Azoreana*. The sharks veered off and disappeared in the darkness.

Up above, the crew were waiting for us. Their sparks had received my message that we were coming over. They tossed out a line, dropped a rope ladder for our unsteady ascent to the deck, and invited us in to the mess for crackers and beer.

The trip paid off: we obtained tools for Frank and me and information for our captain. Fishing, right here, couldn't be beat—about as much as we could handle, they said.

Fishing At Last

Early next morning Manuel Blanco started chumming. Huge smooth swirls appeared in the water where the tuna rose to the bait and dived without breaking surface.

"Three-pole!" shouted Manuel. He could instantly distinguish between small, medium, and large tuna by the size and contour of the swirl.

The entire crew broke for the fishing walkways in pre-assigned groups of three. One from each group was responsible for collecting and distributing a pole to each member, with all three lines tied to a single hook. John placed me between himself and Manuel Rodriguez in the metal cage just off the port stern. We swung the shiny hook above us in concert, and slapped it into the smooth, welling sea. In a flash the hook was taken by a huge tuna, rising from below, headed straight into the air. A firm tug set the hook and all three poles bent to guide the fish along its upward arc, propelled by its own energy, landing on the deck behind us with a thud. Instantly our hook freed itself, and we slapped it down into the water again, ready for the next bite.

The same sequence happened all along the side of the boat. Often three or four big tuna were in the air at the same time, each weighing over two hundred fifty pounds. When the deck filled up, one group of fishermen would break out and drag the fish by the tail, sliding it with a splash into the refrigerated hold below.

I learned a lesson the first time I helped with this chore. A big tuna's body slims down to less than an inch just in front of its caudal fin, making it easy to grab onto with two fingers and pull the heavy fish along the slippery deck. But you do this at your own peril. While still alive, the tail hits the deck in hard, rapid sequence, rat-tat-tatting like a machine gun.

When I casually picked up a big tuna to pull it out of the way, it suddenly came alive and whacked my fingers into the deck, leaving them painful and bleeding. After that, I kicked each body to be sure it was dead before dragging it to the hold.

Blood from the fishing operation attracted sharks. They would cruise up and down along the boat, beneath our feet. Occasionally one would catch onto a hook accidentally and have to be brought aboard for untangling. The danger here was keeping out of reach of the undulating swaths of motion of a shark's body on deck, so different from the sharp, repetitive snapping motion of a tuna's tail. Henry showed me a vicious slice he had received on a previous trip when a shark's tooth cut deeply into the base of his thumb when he was trying to remove the hook. He didn't blame the shark.

It was a wondrous day for fishing. Before calling it quits, we caught twenty-five tons of tuna. "Keep this up," the captain urged, "and we'll be able to head home in less than ten days!" He was exultant. At the dinner table, everybody was exhausted, but excitement and expectations were high. Nothing could stop us now.

TO WHOM IT MAY CONCERN:

THE HOLDER, ROBERT A. NORDYKE, RADIO OPERATOR ON THE M.V.MADEIRENSE, INJURED HIS ARM WHILE FISHING NEAR REDONDO ROCK, GALAPAGOS ISLANDS, SUNDAY MORNING, SEPTEMBER 14, 1941. ACCORDING TO INFORMATION RECEIVED FROM THE U. S. MARINE HOSPITAL IN SAN FRANCISCO, AND AS VERIFIED BY DR. LUIS CELLERI OF SAN CRISTOBAL ISLAND, GALAPAGOS, THE ARM IS BROKEN AND IN NEED OF IMMEDIATE MEDICAL ATTENTION. EXCERPT FROM TELEGRAM FROM U.S.M.H.: "MAKE FOR NEAREST PORT FOR X-RAY AND PROPER MEDICAL CARE."

WE ARE SENDING HIM TO SAN DIEGO ON THE FIRST AVAILABLE BOAT.

SIGNED *Antonio Francisco*
MASTER, M.V.MADEIRENSE

"A large tuna hit our hook, pulling my right arm against the railing with a loud snap. The pain was immediate and intense. 'Maybe it's broke!' Frank said."

The next day we caught twenty tons. On the third day the fish continued to bite, one after the other. At about noon an unfortunate thing happened. A large tuna hit our hook, but, instead of the usual upward soaring, it suddenly turned downward, pulling my right arm against the railing with a loud snap. The pain was immediate and intense. John and Manuel dropped their poles and helped me up onto the deck where we examined my arm.

It was distorted. A deep concavity started at the wrist and extended nearly to the elbow. Frank, the engineer, came up from below when he heard the cry.

"I know what that is!" he said confidently. "It's out of place. All you have to do is pull, and it'll drop back where it belongs. I've seen that before."

So Frank held on to my hand while John grabbed onto the arm above the elbow, and with a one-two-three they yanked with all their might. It hurt, excruciatingly. Nothing changed. They yanked again. It hurt, even worse. No change.

"Maybe it's broke," Frank said. "Probably shouldn't pull any more."

I agreed.

Piper Cub.

Lockheed Lodestar.

Boeing B-17G "Flying Fortress".

Chapter Eight

ᛝ AIRPLANES ᛝ

The Piper Cub

It was a lazy Sunday afternoon in 1944 at Eglin Air Force Base on the southwestern coast of the Florida panhandle. Jack Peterson and I were strolling along outside the hangar when Richard Forst, a veteran pilot recently returned from forty-two sorties on the North African front, called out to us, asking if we'd like to take a whirl up over the swampland and across to Pensacola in a Piper Cub, just for the fun of it. The little plane was a four-seater, maintained to amuse the pilots of big bombers in their time off.

We had nothing else to do, so why not? Richard pulled out three parachutes from their bins in the hangar, tossed one to each of us and took one himself. Together we released the lines that lashed the airplane to the apron to keep it from flopping around in the wind, and climbed in. Dick settled into the pilot's position front-left and began clicking on the startup switches. I slid into the seat directly behind him. Jack was the last to climb in, taking the co-pilot's position front-right. We snapped on our seat belts and adjusted the parachutes.

The single propeller whirred and the plane began to move out, bumping slowly along the ramp toward the far end of the broad landing strip that was intended for heavy warplanes. Leaning forward I could easily watch the indicators for engine speed, air speed, elevation off the ground, and a myriad of other interesting gauges, and see clearly through the sloping front window past the pilot to the action ahead.

At the end of the runway Richard pressed one brake, spun the plane around into starting position, got clearance from the tower to take off, cocked his head, confidently smiled, and gave us the thumbs-up sign. He revved the engine, released the brakes, and accelerated down the concrete strip, pressing me tightly against the seat.

The air speed indicator needle advanced steadily from forty to fifty to sixty miles an hour. Takeoff usually occurred at an air speed of seventy-five or eighty, Dick had told us, so I was comfortably settled back waiting for the wheels to lift off the ground. We were about to become airborne.

But abruptly, still on the ground, the little plane swerved to the right, aiming directly across the wide runway, barreling straight towards its tree-lined edge at seventy-five miles an hour. What's the matter with Richard? What's he doing? We're going fast enough to rise off the ground but we can't possibly clear the trees!

*Military
identification
cards*

Quickly the edge loomed closer, the trees were directly ahead, and the speed indicator stayed at seventy-five! What the heck is he doing? We were plowing straight into the woods, still on the ground. My heart was pounding.

At the last possible moment before the inevitable crash, the plane whipped to the left, aiming sharply up the far edge of the runway, leaning hard. Brakes shrieked, wings and fuselage shook, and the small plane shuddered to a stop.

Dead silence. Richard, perspiring and red-faced, leaned down and picked up a black object on the floor in front of him. With a trembling hand he displayed it to us. It was the heel from his right shoe that had caught between the rudder control and the floor. In the last seconds of the aborted flight he was able to apply superhuman strength, yank back his foot, break the heel off his shoe, and release the rudder.

Sheepishly he pulled off the shoe with a missing heel for us to see. If the heel had been more tightly nailed to the shoe, it might have cost us our lives.

Richard was happy it broke off.

So were we. All of us smiled.

Capt. Robert A. Nordyke, U.S. Air Force, 1942–1946.

Lockheed Lodestar

My job at Eglin Field was instructor in an Officers' School for Radar Countermeasures (radar jamming). In that capacity I got extra pay for flying hours, and had to get them in each month.

Passing by the hangar one early afternoon I met John Petrowski, a pilot friend, who said he was about to leave for a flight to Shreveport in one of the A-29 Lockheed Lodestars. It would be just for fun. We'd see the city and be back for supper. His heavy parachute was draped over one shoulder and he was on his way out to the plane to take off in a few minutes. If I wanted to go, all I had to do was to sign out a parachute and climb aboard. He'd wait. Hurry!

I rushed into the hangar to pick up a parachute. The sergeant in charge was unusually slow, seeming to fumble getting my name, serial number, and size, pawing into cubicle after cubicle trying to find a parachute that would fit. Finally he got it straight, and shoved his choice of a chute across the counter to me. His whole attitude was irritatingly bureaucratic, even surly.

I grabbed the chute, letting the sergeant feel my indignation at his slowness. Why couldn't he be more efficient? What kind of enlisted men do we have these days? Dashing out to the runway, breathless, to my dismay I saw the plane moving out. John hadn't waited for me. I shouted and waved frantically and ran out on the runway towards the plane, hoping he'd see me and stop long enough to pick me up. No luck.

With acute disappointment I slowly retraced my steps to the hangar and—to the sergeant's disgust—dumped the parachute on the counter and signed it back in. I started dejectedly towards my quarters, feeling anger towards the sergeant for being so interminably slow, and feeling abandoned by John who promised to take me with him. I watched the Lodestar rumble down the runway and lift off smoothly. It made me sick to be left behind. They'd have fun in Shreveport.

What happened then is indelibly written on my mind. The airplane slowly gained altitude as it curved back over the base, tipping its wings to say goodbye. Suddenly it turned over in front of my eyes, nosed straight into the ground, and blew up in a great billow of fire, scattering metal parts in every direction.

All fourteen bodies were charred beyond recognition. No one survived. I was appointed officer-in-charge to identify the young men, including John, notify their loved ones, and send off the belongings left in their barracks.

Jamming Orlando

The four-engine B-17 bomber was loaded with electronic jamming equipment and "windows" (strips of aluminum cut to radar frequencies, dropped into the sky to simulate blips on radar screens that looked like airplanes, aimed at eliminating their gun-laying ability). We were about to take off as part of an Air Force training mission to determine how well we could jam a radar station near Orlando, keeping it from "seeing" our airplane, and wiping out its ability to locate us.

The pilot cleared with the tower for take-off and announced over the intercom that we were on our way for a great day. The big bomber lumbered down the runway, rose gently into the air, banked over the edge of the Gulf of Mexico, and turned eastward across the lush swampland towards Orlando, a beautiful city full of little lakes in the middle of Florida's peninsula.

Our target radar was perched on top of a rounded hill that rose four hundred feet above the surrounding swamps several miles south of Orlando. As we approached the site from two thousand feet above, we could clearly see its spiked antenna sticking up from the center building. Its crisscrossed metal arms turned and followed us as we passed overhead.

Our pilot conversed with the site by radio. He let them know we were about to turn on our electronic jammers and let "windows" flutter out behind. They responded that they were ready, and challenged us to do our best to incapacitate their ability to aim guns.

CAPTAIN ROBERT A. NORDYKE   0 858 002

To you who answered the call of your country and served in its Armed Forces to bring about the total defeat of the enemy, I extend the heartfelt thanks of a grateful Nation. As one of the Nation's finest, you undertook the most severe task one can be called upon to perform. Because you demonstrated the fortitude, resourcefulness and calm judgment necessary to carry out that task, we now look to you for leadership and example in further exalting our country in peace.

Harry Truman

The Nordyke siblings, 1945.
Jim (U.S. Navy) and Bob (U.S. Air Force), standing;
Betty and Helen, sitting.

A call on the intercom from the pilot signaled the countermeasures officers to start the action. Excitement was pervasive.

We flipped on the jammer boxes and opened tubes in the tail of the B-17 to let "windows" stream into the turbulent air behind us, all designed to hide ourselves from the radar's view. After half an hour of jamming, the ground crew called to say their screens had never been so completely and so steadily blanked out. Our pilot was pleased, and he transmitted the good news to those of us operating the equipment. We gave a sigh of relief. All our weeks of planning and preparation had paid off handsomely.

As a last gesture of thanks, the pilot decided to buzz the radar site by sliding up on the hill from below, skimming over the tower, and tipping his wings in a friendly goodbye.

Watching out of the window I could see that we were too close to the ground. Suddenly an immense pressure sank me deeply into the seat, taking my breath away. Within seconds the plane jerked and tossed me against the seat ahead. Then it lurched forward, pinning me back into my seat. Finally the jerking motions stopped, and we all sat quietly, stunned, shaking our heads, trying to make sense out of what happened. The plane rose into the air, leveled off, and flew silently across the marshes to Eglin Field.

The landing was rough. We taxied up to the hangar and all of us quickly jumped out. One view of the tail told the whole story. Sticking out from the horizontal and vertical tail fins were long metal radar antenna arms. The approach to the hill had been too low. The pilot didn't calculate on the antenna. When he suddenly recognized the problem, he wrenched the huge bomber into a steep climb to clear the antenna, but it was too late. Its wires caught in the tail and yanked our plane to a near stop before the antenna broke off at barely enough speed to continue flight.

The pilot apologized. Ten of us crew were thankful to be home.

*Jim and Bob with
the "new" and old
flat bed trucks they
bought for their trash
hauling business
in Berkeley and
Oakland, California.*

Chapter Nine

⳵ TRASH HAULING ⳵

It was 1945. The Battle of the Bulge in France and the atomic bombs that flattened Hiroshima and Nagasaki were lingering bad dreams. World War II was over. I had been discharged from the Air Force as a captain, with the GI Bill of Rights in hand that would provide schooling of my choice for the time equal to time-in-service—forty-two months. I figured that should be enough to get me through pre-med and medical school, if handled right.

Brother Jim was soon to be discharged from the U.S. Navy as a Lieutenant, JG, and he wanted to go to Forestry School and work in the woods. In preparation for entering the University of California, Jim and I pooled our military savings and bought a house at 744 Keeler Avenue in Berkeley for Mother (and later ourselves) to live in. It was a nice little home on a winding street near the top of Grizzly Peak, looking out across the San Francisco Bay. On clear nights you could see the glittering lights of Berkeley and San Francisco; at other times, especially in summer, the fog rolled in across the Bay, creeping up the hills until it enshrouded us with its cool, moist fingers.

That was enchanting, but the trouble was we had no visible means of support except for the GI Bill, which wouldn't be enough to pay the monthly mortgage after covering bills for food, tuition, and books.

Harry

While sunning myself on the front lawn one day, I observed interesting movements next door at the home of Harry Jones. Two rough-looking fellows in a battered truck squealed their brakes down his steep driveway, jumped out, and together forked a pile of tree cuttings onto the high-walled truck. As they reversed back up the driveway, extended branches scraped the eaves of the house, scattering leaves in all directions. The men stopped at the top only long enough to collect a check from Harry. The whole operation took less than fifteen minutes.

I sauntered over to where Harry was raking up the leaves the men left behind on the driveway and engaged him in conversation. Harry was a tall, lean, strikingly good-looking fellow in his early thirties, full of confidence and good humor, who got along well with the girls ("Let's lie down and talk about it!"). His second wife, Jill, became a well known artist. Harry was wily in the ways of the world, and he owned a number of rental units in Berkeley. In the past he had told me of devious ways to get around the rent control laws ("Charge them extra for an old refrigerator!").

"How much did you pay those guys for that job?" I asked.

"Fifteen dollars."

"Fifteen dollars! I can't believe it. They were here only fifteen minutes. I timed them."

"That's what they ask, and I'm quite willing to pay them to get rid of the big pile of rubbish in my backyard," Harry said.

I pressed him. "Suppose Jim and I wanted to do that. How hard is it to get started?"

"Easy. Just get a business license from the city for $2.50, buy yourself a truck, send out some advertising, and off you go. You can begin with me. I'll have another pile of trash and trimmings ready for you in a couple of weeks. Believe me, it's easy. If you put on a good front, do a nice job, and clean up well after yourself, you'll make a mint," he smiled reassuringly.

I wasn't sure about the mint, but the idea of trash hauling sounded promising, especially since it might be flexible enough to allow Jim and me to go to school and carry on the business between classes. Good physical exercise, too, while paying the mortgage.

Bob, a graduate student in pre-medicine, Sather Gate, UC Berkeley, 1946. "School, intertwined with trash hauling, seemed to be an unbeatable combination. Life was almost exhilarating both mentally and physically."

• G E N E R A L   H A U L I N G •

NORDYKE BROTHERS
(Veterans)

Rubbish-Trimmings, Light Local Moving

Permit 788   AShberry 6859

*Business calling card
for trash hauling.*

Getting Started

Jim was still awaiting discharge from the Navy, but by quick correspondence we agreed on our new business. I paid for the license and bought a 1925 Chevrolet with a flat bed for $75.00. As soon as he arrived home, we attached wooden sides that rose six feet off the truck bed and built a back gate that could hold the load in place while bouncing down the road.

Now we had the equipment. The next challenge was to find some business.

First, we designed and printed calling cards. Then we distributed them personally to over two hundred homes in the wealthier part of the Berkeley hills by walking up and down the streets, ringing doorbells, handing out cards, and explaining that we were veterans just out of the war trying to work our way through college (both strong pluses those days).

Responses were all pleasant but negative. "I'm sorry I don't need your services now, but I'll keep your card in case I do."

Jobs

For weeks nothing happened. Jim and I started classes, and Mother stood by the telephone, in case someone called.

Then the rings began. One after another person requested hauling of their rubbish. We took turns estimating jobs. Small ones paid ten to twenty dollars, some larger ones brought up to fifty dollars! At first we worked together lifting trash onto the truck. Later we found it more efficient for one of us to load up between classes and leave the truck parked on a street; the other would break out in his spare time, drive it to the Berkeley dump, and pitch off the load.

There was no cost to dump trash originating in Berkeley, but rubbish from anyplace else was charged a dollar. We were constantly arguing with the often obnoxious guard about where our trash came from. Our usual name for him was "BB" for Big Boss, but it became "Pieface" in disrespectful undertones when he especially disturbed us.

San Francisco–Oakland Bay Bridge.
"I pressed my foot on the gas pedal of the old truck and tore across the Bay Bridge . . . "
[for an interview at the University of California Medical School].

The Interview

School, intertwined with trash hauling, seemed to be an unbeatable combination. Life was almost exhilarating both mentally and physically, and we were at least holding our heads above water economically. What could be better than that?

I had applied to a number of medical schools (Yale, St. Louis, NYU, Stanford, and the University of California). In my mind Cal headed the list since it was near home, relatively inexpensive, and (I was told) as good as the others.

Yale answered early and required $25 to hold the slot, so I sent them a check to be sure I got in somewhere, even though I knew the cost would be excessive. The plan then was to shift sidewise, always retaining one acceptance until a more desirable one was cinched down. St. Louis asked if I really wanted to go there. I told them no. On March 5, Stanford, my second choice, requested $50 to hold a position—payable by April first. That was a lot of money. I decided to hold off paying it until the last minute before it was due, hoping against hope that Cal would come through.

After what seemed an unbearably long time, a letter came from Cal requesting an interview with Dr. Gliebe, a psychiatrist known for his bluntness. The meeting would be critically important.

A week later, at 2:30 in the afternoon, I was daydreaming my way along the bumpy road winding out of the dump, sweating and dirty, when suddenly I remembered that my

UNIVERSITY OF CALIFORNIA

OFFICE OF THE DEAN
MEDICAL SCHOOL
THE MEDICAL CENTER
SAN FRANCISCO 22, CALIFORNIA

April 17, 1947

Mr. Robert A. Nordyke
744 Keeler Avenue
Berkeley 8, California

Dear Mr. Nordyke:

With reference to your application for admission to the
September, 1947 class of the Medical School, I am glad to
inform you that you will be accepted for that class. Nat-
urally, your admission will be subject to the satisfactory
completion of our requirements unless, of course, you have
completed the requirements already.

Will you please send your check or money order in the
amount of $50.00 to the Director of Admissions, University
of California, Berkeley 4. This represents a deposit on
your admission.

With all good wishes,

Sincerely yours,

Francis Scott Smyth, M.D.
Dean

FSS/z

cc- University Admissions Director
    Dr. C. A. Noble, Jr.
    Dean E. C. Voorhies

STANFORD UNIVERSITY
ADMISSION CERTIFICATE
GRADUATE DIVISION

Date *April 10, 1947*

Mr. *Robert A. Nordyke*
744 Keeler Ave.
Berkeley 8, California

Your application for admission to Stanford University has been favorably considered and
you will be allowed to matriculate on *September 30, 1947* in the
Graduate Division for work in the *School of Medicine* if
you fulfill the conditions stipulated below prior to that date, and are present before 5 p.m. on
that day.

The conditions which you must fulfill are checked below:

1. Complete work in progress with satisfactory grades and forward official report to this
office, if possible before *August 15, 1947*

2. Graduate from college.

This statement applies to this date only and does not assure admission at any other time.
A renewal of application for a subsequent quarter will be considered in competition with all
other applications for that quarter.

John M. Stalnaker
Chairman, Committee on Admissions

Please bring this certificate with you when registering.

FORM 25 C

---

interview with Dr. Gliebe was scheduled for 3 o'clock at the University of California
Hospital, high up on Mt. Parnassus on the far side of San Francisco. My heart thumped
and I could feel my face redden. How could I have forgotten that? What to do? Should I
drive home, wash up, and change my clothes? That would, for sure, make me late. Should
I just race over the way I was? What would he think of me in this condition?

I made the decision on the spot: go for it. So I pressed my foot on the gas pedal of the
old truck and tore across the Bay Bridge. The wind was strong, blowing hard against its
high, rickety, wooden sides. The swaying made it difficult to stay in one lane. Off the
ramp in San Francisco, I raced up Market Street, hoping against hope for green lights all
the way. No luck. I arrived at the hospital at ten minutes after three.

There was no obvious parking place, so I double parked, left the key in the truck,
jumped out, and dashed up the steps to the rotunda. Dr. Gliebe's name was on a long
list: second floor, room 245. I bounced up the stairs and ran down the corridor. Glancing
at room signs, I nearly collided with a balding, stocky man emerging from room 245. He
was firmly clicking the door shut behind him and donning a fedora hat.

"Are you Nordyke?"

"Yes, sir."

"Why are you late?"

"Well, sir . . . "

"I asked you, why are you late?"

"Well, sir, I was hauling trash in Berkeley when . . ."

"You were what?" he said gruffly, searching his pocket for a key and opening the door again.

"Come in. Sit down. Tell me about it."

He took off his hat, pointed to a chair, and we began to talk.

"Tell me again why you were late. I don't think I understood you."

We talked on for nearly an hour. The main subjects were trash hauling, the economics of taking care of a mother while going to school, riding the top of box cars through Sierra tunnels, fighting forest fires in Montana. Nothing about medicine.

Together we walked out, he with his hat, jacket, and tie, I with my dirty jeans, tousled hair, and open shirt. It was a relief that there was no ticket on the window of the truck.

An acceptance to the UC School of Medicine arrived ten days later.

New Truck

As business grew, the limitations of our old Chevrolet truck became apparent. It was just as hard to unload as to load it, doubling the work. At the dump we had to climb on top, use pitchforks and shovels to toss off the loads, often getting scratched and tangled in branches. Anyway, it was too small for the size jobs we were getting and we'd often have to make several trips when one should have been enough.

Fortunately the Army was selling military trucks to veterans at auction in Oakland. Jim and I attended a sale and became proud owners of a 1 1/2 ton olive drab GI truck. We drove it to an auto shop and had a power lift installed. The whole thing, truck and lift, came to $985. There were double wheels behind, a four-wheel drive, and only a few dents. When the motor was running, you could just push a button on the dashboard, up would go the truck bed, and (wonder of wonders) off would slide the entire load. Oh, the beauty of it!

The only mishap occurred when Jim and I were coasting down wide, palm-lined Euclid Avenue in Berkeley with a big load of branches and I accidentally bumped against the button. We didn't notice it ourselves, but a passing driver angrily yelled at us. Looking through the mirror we saw the back tilted up and trash littering the street, extending for nearly a block. It took us half an hour to pick up the load and leave the street clean.

Lonely Lady

Now and again, when business slackened, Jim and I would print up some new cards and go house to house in areas we hadn't visited before, knocking on doors and introducing ourselves. One of these houses stands out in my memory more than the others.

I rang the doorbell of the expansive, gabled home several times, waited, heard nothing, and started to walk down the steps. Just then the door cracked open and an attractive middle-aged woman called out: "What is it you want?" Her voice sounded impatient.

"Here is my card," I said, bounding back up the stairs. "My brother and I are veterans working our way through college by hauling trash, cuttings, or anything else you might want taken away."

She read the card slowly, her mind seeming off in the distance. "I may have something for you. Come back tomorrow afternoon at three."

The next day I arrived promptly at three and rang the doorbell. She came out, led me down a steep, corrugated driveway to a basement door on the side of the house. It was dark inside. She switched on a small light that barely illuminated a long couch and a pile of boxes at the edge of the basement wall.

"Let's sit down here a minute." She motioned to the couch. "What would you charge to take away all those boxes?"

The aroma of perfume emanated from her low-cut dress and the scent of alcohol was clearly evident from her breath as she sat on the couch next to me.

"My husband is away in San Francisco, but he leaves these kinds of things to me. He wouldn't care how much it cost." She moved closer.

I was suddenly uncomfortable. This was not about trash hauling any more. I wasn't quite sure what it was about, but I quickly rose, groped through the darkened basement for the closed door, and made my way into the bright afternoon sunshine.

From then on we bypassed the house of the lonely lady.

Contract Hauling

After two years of combining school and trash hauling, we needed to make a decision. School was tougher and more demanding and the trash business had escalated beyond our ability to keep up with it. Still, we needed the money.

An opportunity arose. Mother spotted an ad in the Oakland Tribune: a large building was being torn down on Broadway in the center of Oakland and the contractors would pay $1,000 a month for a truck and driver to help haul away the debris. It sounded just right for us.

744 Keeler Avenue

Berkeley 8, Calif.

November 1, 1948

Dear Customer:

    This year the pressure of studies has increased to the point where Nordyke Brothers must give up their hauling business in order to devote all of their time to studying. Bob is in San Francisco now, in the second year of Medical School, and Jim is a senior in the Forestry School here in Berkeley. We have appreciated your business over these past two years and we have enjoyed working for you.

    For your future hauling needs we would like to recommend Whitcher Brothers, whose card we are enclosing for your convenience. They have been located here in Berkeley for the past year, and we feel that they will give you good hauling service at a reasonable price.

Very sincerely yours,

Bob Nordyke

Jim Nordyke

Letter of resignation from the trash hauling business.

So we hired a young fellow as a driver eight hours a day, five days a week, for $150 a month. His job was to drive our truck under the end of a wooden chute where pieces of broken concrete and splintered boards slid onto the truck from above in a cloud of dust. When the truck filled up, he would drive to the Berkeley dump, pay "Pieface" a dollar, pull over to the assigned dumping place, push the lift button, slide the load onto the pile, and return to the building. It was easy for the driver, and good for us —our first taste of entrepreneurship.

That job lasted six months. We netted about $750 a month after paying the driver, truck, and dumping costs—pretty good for those days, and a lot easier for us.

Addendum

Five years later, after graduating from UC San Francisco School of Medicine, I was interning at the Kaiser-Permanente Hospital in Oakland. During one month on the obstetrics service I delivered, under supervision, eighty babies. Near the end of that rotation one of the obstetricians had delivered a normal baby and asked me to move in and finish sewing up the episiotomy. After the final stitch, I tipped back my mask, looked at the woman from between her draped and spread-out legs, and told her that all was well and her baby was beautiful.

She looked me straight in the eye and said, "Aren't you my trash man?"

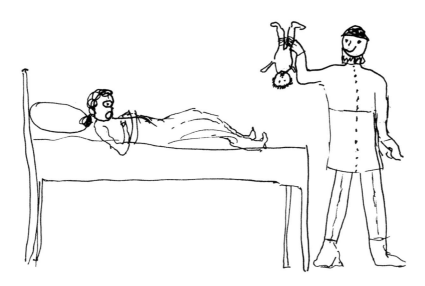

"Aren't you my trash man?"

Courting days, 1948.

Chapter Ten

ᖇᖇ ELLIE ᖇᖇ

The Meeting

My first recognition that a charming young lady named Ellie Cole was about to enter my universe and stay there until death do us part, or beyond, came in the year 1947. The story is hard to believe, and even a bit embarrassing to me, but it's true.

After graduating from Berkeley and spending four years as a radar countermeasures officer in the Air Force, I returned home to enter pre-med and medical school while brother Jim entered Forestry School. We combined funds and energies for a down payment on a house at 741 Keeler Avenue in the Berkeley hills to provide a place to live for our mother and us.

Then ensued an erratic series of girl friends that my mother didn't approve of. I thought they were fun, but none was right for a permanent relationship, or even close to it, and she thought at the age of twenty-eight, it was high time I settled down. So did I.

One Sunday afternoon my mother and I were casually sitting at the kitchen table gazing out across the fog of the San Francisco Bay as it curled up the hillside towards our house. She began the conversation that led to my setting up a grid on a piece of paper, listing down one side a series of attributes that a wife should have and across the other side a series of all the girls' names who were reasonable possibilities for a wife. The attributes included (as I remember them) thoughtfulness, energy, independence, humor, education, beauty, a strong family. Across the top were the names of six or seven girls who had been culled from a larger number, and in each little box was a number from 1 to 10.

After the adding and subtracting, lo! Ellie Cole's name led all the rest.

Let's go see her!

So we called her home in San Jose. Her surprised father, Ralph G. Cole, told me she was working at a summer job as a leader at a Girl Scout Camp in the Santa Cruz mountain redwoods at Big Basin.

Within the hour we were on our way. From there on the story gets a little hazy. According to Ellie's account, the camp director came to her cabin to report the arrival of a visitor.

"There's a young man by the name of Bob Nordyke and his mother who would like to see you," she said.

Ellie only vaguely remembered Bob Nordyke as the older brother of her high school

A GRID FOR SELECTING A LIFE PARTNER

Attributes for a Wife	Rose	Priscilla	Ellie	Mary Ann	Ethel	Beth
Thoughtfulness	10	8	10	10	8	9
Energy	5	8	9	8	9	10
Independence	8	9	9	8	8	10
Humor	8	7	9	9	7	9
Intelligence	8	7	10	9	8	9
Education	9	8	10	10	8	9
Beauty	10	10	10	10	10	10
Strong family relationship	8	5	10	7	8	8
Good sport	10	8	10	10	9	9
Same religion	9	2	10	10	10	2
Love of music	5	8	9	5	5	10
Total	90	80	106	96	90	95

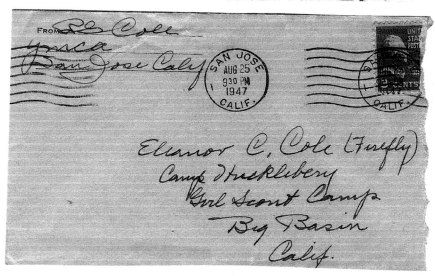

A letter sent to Ellie at Huckleberry Girl Scout Camp
from her Dad mentions a possible visit by Bob Nordyke.

Engaged to be married, 1949

and church friend, Jim Nordyke. She arranged to go with us to a Big Basin State Park campfire. I sat down quietly beside her as the program proceeded, without comment. Even to this day Ellie remembers a tingling feeling that she knew she was sitting beside her husband that evening at that campfire. In any case she was the charming self I've learned to love over the years.

> Do you know, Ellie [Antonia], I think of you more than of anyone else in this part of the world. I'd have liked to have you for a sweetheart, or a wife, or my mother or my sister—anything that a woman can be to a man. The idea of you is a part of my mind; you influence my likes and dislikes, all my tastes, hundreds of times when I don't realize it. You really are a part of me.
>
> *Paraphrased from* My Antonia *by Willa Cather, 1926:321.*

Wedding day

Roses

Ellie and I were married on June 18, 1950. That date was chosen because it was her graduation day at Stanford and Ellie's mother wouldn't let her get married until she graduated.

Starting one year later, a tradition developed: I always surprised her with a dozen roses on our wedding anniversary. Each time she was filled with wonder and let me know how she didn't expect it but how pleased she was. It never failed. The deeper the tradition became entrenched, the greater the requirement to carry it out.

On the evening of Saturday, June 17, 1978, Ellie and I and three children were happily cruising northward out of France in our rented VW van. It was the beginning of a six-week camping trip through Europe. Excitement was in the air. Everybody was in agreement on which route to take. Each person had a chance to vote, Father made the decisions. Our plan was to be in Germany tonight, then camp through Belgium, Holland, and England.

As we were winding along through the fading light of the forested countryside, an unexplained anxiety began to grow and I became a bit testy. Then it dawned on me. Tomorrow was Sunday the 18th, it was our anniversary, we would be in Germany, florist shops were closed, and money couldn't be changed anyway. No roses. Dejection set in.

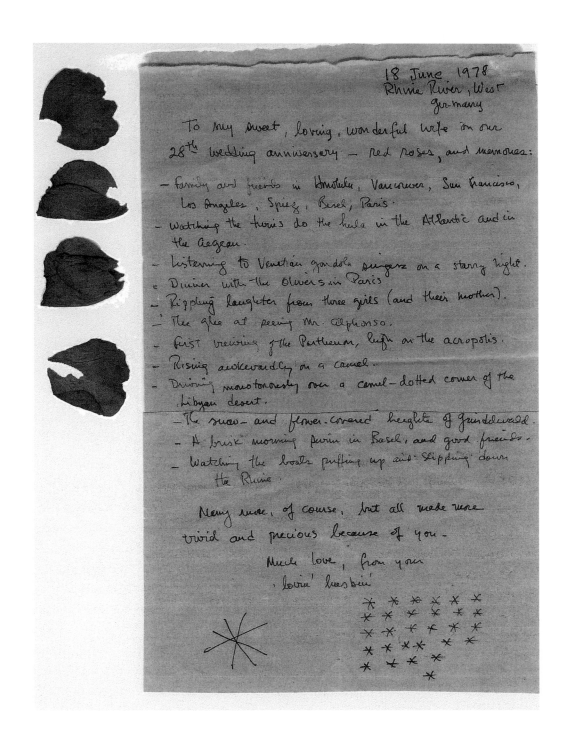

18 June 1978
Rhine River, West
Germany

To my sweet, loving, wonderful wife on our
28th wedding anniversary — Red roses, and memories:

- Family and friends in Honolulu, Vancouver, San Francisco,
  Los Angeles, Spiez, Basel, Paris.
- Watching the turns do the hula in the Atlantic and in
  the Aegean.
- Listening to Venetian gondola singers on a starry night.
- Dinner with the Olivers in Paris
- Rippling laughter from three girls (and their mother).
- The glee at seeing Mr. Alphonso.
- First viewing of the Parthenon, high on the acropolis.
- Rising awkwardly on a camel.
- Driving monotonously over a camel-dotted corner of the
  Libyan desert.
- The snow- and flower-covered heights of Grindelwald.
- A brisk morning swim in Basel, and good friends.
- Watching the boats puffing up and slipping down
  the Rhine.

Many more, of course, but all made more
vivid and precious because of you.

Much love, from your
'lovin' husbin'

Anniversary, June 18, 1978.
"A tradition developed: I always surprised her with a dozen roses on our wedding anniversary."
Rose petals from our campsite along the Rhine River.

Anniversary, June 18, 1985, Lake Tahoe, California.

Across the border we rolled, through the gate of our German campground, pulled into an assigned space, got out and stretched. The light was dim, but what was that? My gosh, what was that?

Rimming the entire camp was a hedge of—of what? RED ROSES. Can't believe it! Hundreds and hundreds. New-formed buds, full-ripened blooms, and faded brown petals softening the pathway.

A terrible dilemma! All my upbringing said, "You can't do that!" All my emotions said, "What a deal!"

With malice aforethought, and against everything my parents ever taught me, I transferred a pair of scissors from Ellie's sewing kit into the back pocket of my jeans.

"It's time for bed now. Be fresh for tomorrow," I directed the family, with a touch of hidden glee.

They clambered into their respective sleeping bags in the van, three on the leveled-out floor space, one in a hammock slung above the two front seats. I crawled in last, on top of a wiggling and objecting tangle of children and wife.

It took a while to settle down. But finally the moon shone softly against clouds in the east-ward sky, the chatter subsided, and heavy breathing was the only sound. Now was the time.

Cautiously I crawled toward the front seat, reached up and clicked open the door handle, waited silently for sounds of awakening, slowly opened the creaky door and slid under the hammock, head first, onto the ground. Shaking the dust off my shirt, I headed towards the bathroom to make it all look legitimate, then sidled to the back of the hedge. Oh, what beautiful red roses!

Furtively, I looked up and down to be sure no one was about, then began quietly snipping stems, one by one. There were hundreds of them. Nobody will miss them, I said to myself, if I take only one here and there. Roses don't live that long, anyway. The owners wouldn't blame me if they knew my purpose.

Six, then eight. The moon drifted out from behind a cloud and poured light directly on me. I stopped, motionless. The moon faded again behind a dark cloud. Ten. The vague outline of a tall man in a bathrobe loomed toward me, carrying a packet. I could hear the crunch of each footstep on the graveled roadway, closer, louder. Had he seen me? Was he coming toward me? He veered off to the bathroom. I waited till he came out and disappeared back toward the campground, steps fading in the distance.

Snip, snip. Twelve. My opened shirt was just loose enough to hide all the roses underneath.

With slight rasping from the thorns on my chest at each step, I sauntered casually back to the van. Groping for the door handle as quietly as possible, I wiggled back inside by rearranging legs and arms, extracted the roses from beneath my shirt, laid them out, and fell fast asleep.

At daybreak—a gasp from Ellie! What's this? It can't be! A blanket of roses! Where did you . . . ? How . . . ? Can't believe it. Surprised. Didn't expect it. So filled with wonder!

Never miss an anniversary, you know!

Bob wrote in June, 1997:
"It turned out to be
as near-perfect a
melding of lives and
loves as it is possible
to imagine."

Anniversary, June 18, 1996, Honolulu, Hawai'i.

APPENDIX

Robert A. Nordyke, M.D., F.A.C.P.
Nuclear Medicine, Straub Clinic, Honolulu, Hawai'i

Professor of Medicine
Chief, Division of Nuclear Medicine
John A. Burns School of Medicine
University of Hawai'i

The family joins Bob at a gathering to celebrate his Straub Clinic retirement in June, 1995.
Back row: *Nalani, Bob, Mary Ellen, and Aimee Grace; Jay, Tom, and Michelle Nordyke;*
DuWayne Worthington; Susan (Nunu) Nordyke.
Middle row: *Cameron Grace; Bob and Ellie Nordyke; Noelle Grace; Larissa and Nica Nordyke;*
Gretchen (Nini) N. and Kaylin Worthington; Trevor Grace.
Front row: *Jennifer, Mike, Carolyn N., and Andy Cozzette; shelties Shani and Kanani.*
Additions since 1995: Mark Worthington (1999), Doug Bell (married Susan, 2002),
and Baby Nordyke Bell (September 2003)

❦ Retirement Speech to Straub Clinic Physicians ❦

ROBERT A. NORDYKE, M.D.

JUNE 26, 1995

I thank Dr. Blake Waterhouse for his kind words of introduction. (I feel like Huckleberry Finn who everyone thought had drowned but who was hiding in the choir loft listening to his eulogy.)

It seems impossible to me that I'm about to retire, but it's true. Someone said retirement should last about two weeks. Mine is going to last about two days.

But I can't deny that I'm getting older and that I'm ready, by most standards, to be put out to pasture. On the day Blake Waterhouse was born, I was taking a course in chemistry at the University of California. That tells you something.

I thought it might be interesting, especially to the younger doctors, to briefly compare what I found when I arrived at Straub in 1960 with what's here now, then look at some of the changes—for better or worse—that have taken place over thirty-five years. Then I would like to modestly suggest an agenda for the future of Straub Clinic & Hospital from one person's point of view. One needs to be careful about prediction, which (to quote Yogi Berra) is difficult, especially about the future.

First—the past. I came to Hawai'i for one reason—my wife, Ellie.

In 1959 we lived in Los Angeles. I was traveling one hundred fifty miles a day over clogged freeways, starting up nuclear medicine services in four hospitals, getting burnt out. Then it happened. Ellie sat on my lap, nibbled on my ear, and said she'd like to return to Hawai'i where she was raised and always considered it to be home. There were no freeways and about the tallest building was the Royal Hawaiian Hotel.

It didn't take much to convince me. So we took a vacation to Hawai'i to look for a job. After chugging for ten hours in an airplane with four propellers, I went to Queen's Hospital and chatted over coffee with a radiologist. He told me that Straub was the best group in town. The Medical Group was pretty good, but Straub was *the best*.

I stopped by the Medical Group anyway, just to check it out. They said they didn't need a specialist in nuclear medicine. In fact, they'd never even heard of it.

So—on to Straub. At the urging of Fred Gilbert and Bob Rigler, who had recently published a paper on the treatment of hyperthyroidism with radioactive iodine, Dr. Stewart Doolittle, the Chief of Medicine, said—maybe . . . But first, my wife had to be checked out. I was told that too many mainlander physicians came here who were good enough doctors, but their wives became homesick, and they soon pulled out. When Dr.

Robert A. Nordyke, M.D.
Straub Clinic, 1960–1995.

Doolittle discovered that Ellie was a Punahou classmate of his son Larry—that cinched the matter!

Straub Clinic was formed in 1921, when I was two years old. Thirty-nine years later I was Straub's thirty-ninth doctor. That's pretty slow going, by present standards.

Among those who greeted me were some old timers who are still with us: Don Jones (two years before), Niall Scully (three years before), and Walter Strode (five years before.

My first office was a little cubby hole carved out of the end of the hall on the third floor of Milnor building. There was one dictating telephone on the floor for four doctors, including John Lowrey, the state's busiest neurosurgeon, who dictated long, detailed reports. I lucked out with Harry Arnold, though. He was the busiest and fastest-moving dermatologist in the state, but he never dictated. He always typed succinct notes with one hand while simultaneously marking up papers for the *Hawaii Medical Journal* that he edited for forty years.

It might be hard for you newer doctors to understand this, but when I first came to Straub in 1960:

- ◆ Patient records were all on little 3x5 cards in packets.
- ◆ There was no such thing as a biochemical profile.
- ◆ There was no CT, MRI, or nuclear imaging.

- There were no women doctors.
- There were no non-Caucasian doctors.
- There were no psychiatrists or psychologists.
- There was no Palma wing.
- There was no hospital.
- There was no research institute or research funding.
- The starting salary was $10,000 per year.
- All partners' salaries were the same, regardless of specialty.
- Pay was recalculated each quarter, depending on collections.
- Fifteen percent of our salary was held aside for future capital.
- To keep physicians out of the state of Hawai'i, a one-year residency was required before licensing. Dr. Alfred S. Hartwell, a cardiologist, followed me around at Queen's Hospital every day to countersign every order for a year.
- Straub had no board of directors. All decisions, large and small, were made by a hand-raising vote in an open forum one night a month.

That may sound bad, but it had some advantages:
- Paper work was minimal.
- Bills were sent out and paid promptly.
- The department of medicine physicians met monthly at each others' homes, sharing information and building lasting friendships.
- There was a deep sense of caring for individual patients that is easy to lose with rapid increase in size and technology.

Well, here we are, thirty-five years later: Hawai'i's population has doubled, freeways fan out every which way, towering concrete smothers the Royal Hawaiian Hotel and Waikiki.

What about Straub? We've gone from thirty-nine to one hundred seventy-five doctors, extending vertically and horizontally.

I'm proud of what we've accomplished in that time:
- Selection of doctors and staff is now based on qualifications regardless of skin color or sex.
- Psychiatry and psychology have become legitimate specialties.
- Our hospital was built and is functioning well.
- I'm glad the widespread practice of smoking is gone.
- I'm glad that primary care/family practice is finally expanding effectively, after a number of aborted tries in the mid-70s.

♦ Our Health Appraisal Center, started in 1965 and operating steadily since, is innovative and preparing to fulfill even greater potential.

♦ Our elected Board of Directors is more organized than was possible under the town hall approach, but the doctors not on the Board sometimes may feel bypassed.

♦ I'm proud that we've kept the same strong vision over the years: a unified, integrated, outpatient and hospital-based, physician-owned system, potentially the most efficient and effective medical care organization in the state. It is the essence of what's needed to take the lead in the upcoming managed care environment.

♦ I'm proud of our development of the best research facilities in Hawai'i for clinical and health services. We have two mature public non-profit research institutes within a few steps of us—the Pacific Health Research Institute and the Straub Foundation. They have grant writers, statisticians, and epidemiologists, and they have access to almost a million dollars a year in research funds that are available for the asking. I'm pleased that we've built them up to their present high level of excellence, and I expect that more Straub doctors will understand the need for research and do it.

♦ I'm especially proud of having some part in the training of more than four hundred students.

Well, if we've accomplished so much, what's left to do? Where do we go from here? (To quote Mark Twain: "Even if you're on the right track, you'll get run over if you just sit there!")

I have a personal list of priorities for the next decade. It might not be the same agenda as yours, but it is distilled from many years of thinking about it. I've culled a longer list down to seven points:

1. We need to carefully but rapidly increase managed care. There is no choice.

2. The use of non-physician personnel should be expanded. With adequate training and supervision, such personnel can often enhance the quantity and quality of patient care while reducing costs and allowing physicians to function more appropriately.

3. We need computerized patient records in every office that can constantly monitor quality, so we'll not only *think* we're the best but be able to *demonstrate* it.

4. Clinical teaching, at every level, needs expanding. On a per-doctor basis, teaching was a greater part of our activities three decades ago than it is now. There are pockets of excellence, of course, as illustrated by Ken Robbins' recent award, but in many other areas we are near the bottom of the list compared to other hospitals. Our agreed-upon written principles say: "Active staff participation in teaching enhances the quality of Straub patient care. We support Straub staff who engage in teaching."

We need to turn more serious attention to teaching, which is so important to ourselves, to our reputation, and to health care throughout the community.

5. My number five priority deals with research. Research is a crucial part of health care, not an ancillary add-on when it's convenient. I didn't say "nice" or "interesting" or "useful." I said *crucial*. It should be carried out continuously in every office and byway to improve quality, contain costs, and improve patient outcomes. Computerized patient records make it much easier. If we can retrieve information acquired at the interface between physician and patient, dozens of questions important to one's own practice can be answered.

6. We must constantly improve personal relationships with our patients individually. This is the final common pathway and the hallmark of Straub. We cannot allow clinic size and technology to get in the way.

7. In the pursuit of excellence, the careful choice of our colleagues makes all the difference. The simple truth is that we must continue to acquire men and women who have the urge to excel. Everything else follows.

I feel incredibly lucky and honored that Straub physicians accepted me to join them despite an unusual new specialty in nuclear medicine, and that you kept me on despite occasional misgivings. It pleases me to think that I may have had some salutary effects on Straub, and Straub certainly has had on me.

In closing, I would be remiss not to thank the following people:
- My mother, who found my wife, Ellie.
- My wife Ellie, who enticed me to Hawaiʻi and produced our five children.
- Our children, who produced eleven beautiful grandchildren, the most recent four weeks ago.
- My colleagues at Straub, who gave me an effective and pleasant workplace and freedom to do what I needed to do.
- The doctors who contributed towards maintaining my good health over the years—Drs. Fred Gilbert, David Andrew, John Balfour, Walter Strode, Bill Hartman, Roger White, Francis Pien, among many others.
- The staffs at Nuclear Medicine, Pacific Health Research Institute, and Straub Foundation, who made it easy to intertwine the practice of medicine with research and teaching.
- The young students, who have invariably taught me more than I have taught them.
- I wish to especially thank Dr. Blake Waterhouse, who has provided us all with a truly

extraordinary quality of leadership, methodically building the infrastructure and the visions that will lead us successfully far into the future.

♦ And, thanks to each one of you for your friendship, collegiality, and steady help over these thirty-five years.

As I start into the new adventures of the last third of my life, Ellie and I wish you all Godspeed.

Ellie and Bob Nordyke wih their sheltie, Shani,
at their home in Mānoa, Honolulu, Hawaiʻi, in 1991.

ꙮ *Commentary* ꙮ

HAWAII MEDICAL JOURNAL, 56:168 (JULY) 1997

ROBERT A. NORDYKE, M.D.

George Chaplin

EDITOR AT LARGE, THE HONOLULU ADVERTISER

Voltaire said, "Men who are occupied in the restoration of health to other men, by the joint exertion of skill and humanity, are above all the great of the earth. They even partake of divinity, since to preserve and renew is almost as noble as to create."

Many of Hawaii's physicians merit such an encomium, but none more than Dr. Robert Nordyke, now seriously ill.

He is well recognized as a pioneer in nuclear medicine, but how many know his background, his formative years that made him into the multi-faceted person that he is?

He arrived 78 years ago in a California farming town, Woodland, in the Sacramento Valley, a town so small the kids could walk to either the elementary or the high school. They had one of each.

It was a time of screened porches and rocking chairs, a time of basic American values. His was a family with little money, but with seven children and lots of love—as well as a tree house that could be reached by climbing out of a second story window and jumping from the roof.

In due course Bob had a broken arm, poison oak and scarlet fever, with a big quarantine sign on the front door and half the family living elsewhere. A lad with standard gustatory priorities, he used to sneak chocolate powder from a large can high on a kitchen shelf. Ever since, he sneezes every time he eats chocolate—either an allergy or an ongoing sense of guilt.

Once, when his parents were away for a day, he was sent to stay with his maternal grandmother. He decided to run away—who among us hasn't?—with pajamas, toothbrush and favorite spinning top in a paper sack. It began to get dark, he was hungry and when a passing policeman told him his mother and dad were looking for him, his resolve melted and he let himself be taken home. Shades of Horatio Alger, Tom Swift and the Rover Boys!

A good, healthy, active American boy, he had his share of problems—from a BB gun that had a habit of shattering windows or targeting a well-padded lady's rump, to a ride on a horse he boldly mounted when he was five years old. The horse stopped on the tracks of the Sacramento Northern Railway and, despite Bob's frantic pleas, refused to budge. Fortunately, the oncoming electric train screeched to a halt just feet away. Meanwhile, his mother was trying to find who had stolen her husband's favorite horse.

While Bob was still young, his dad taught him how to drive the family car. But instead of low gear he put it into reverse and promptly took out a nearby fence.

One summer during the Depression, he picked apricots on a ranch just out of town. He worked 10 hours a day, at 10 cents an hour, with 10 cents deducted for a sandwich and flavored water. Lunch! Incidentally, 10 cents is what it took in those days for a Saturday matinee featuring Tom Mix or Hoot Gibson.

As the Depression wore on, his mother, a Mills College alumna, had to take a job teaching. But it was in a nearly abandoned goldmine town in the Sierra foothills. There were only five children living there and since nine youngsters were required to qualify for an elementary school, Bob and three of his six brothers and sisters had to move there into a broken-down, unpainted shambles of a house, complete with well and outhouse. But winter snow and some old skis they found made up for the hardships.

Let's move to 1939, when at 19 Bob finished his junior year at Berkeley. His four-hour-a-day job in the university library didn't really enable him to save any money, so he got a summer job as a logger, felling timber in the Sierras. He and 17 others were signed up by a persuasive union representative. The next morning they were summarily fired. The National Labor Relations Board reinstated them, but a day later they were fired again— for "not working hard enough." No one since ever accused Bob of that!

A co-worker and friend of Bob's suggested they go to his family's farm in Idaho and pitch hay. Sounded good, but no money for travel, and a thousand miles to go. So, they hopped freight cars, sometimes clambering on top and stretching out, sometimes climbing into empty cars, scrounging food when they could, and most importantly, dodging unfriendly hoboes and railroad police, the notorious "bulls" eager to use their heavy clubs.

They finally got there and made the hay fly. But, always eager for new experiences, Bob during part of that summer worked as a Forest Service firefighter battling wild fires, which are always treacherous, often quick to reverse direction.

He survived, hitchhiked home and was graduated from Berkeley in 1940, having majored in English literature, political science and public speaking.

He signed up with his draft board, and followed with a two-month course in San Francisco in radio repair and radio telegraphy. He then thumbed his way to San Diego and got a job as radio operator on a large tuna fishing boat manned by Portuguese, only three of whom spoke any English.

Off they sailed to the waters of Costa Rica and the Galapagos Islands. He sent Morse Code, up to 30 words a minute!

Came the war and Captain Robert Allan Nordyke put in four years in radar countermeasures. Next, med school at the University of California, San Francisco on the

A section of UCSF Medical School Class of 1951. Bob sits in first row, third from left.

GI Bill. But there was no money to pay for the mortgage on a house he and brother Jim, a Navy lieutenant fresh from service, bought for their mother and themselves in Berkeley.

So he and Jim bought a 1925—repeat, 1925—Chevy with a flat bed for $75 and went into the trash-hauling business in between classes. They did well and soon graduated to a one-and-a-half-ton surplus army truck bought at an auction.

Five years later, when interning at the Kaiser Permanente Hospital in Oakland, Bob Nordyke delivered, under supervision, 80 babies in a single month. Near the end of that rotation, at one delivery, he took off his mask and looked up at the new mother from between her draped legs and told her that all was well and that she had a beautiful baby.

She looked him straight in the eye and then, puzzled and upset, she said, "Aren't you my trash man?"

A few words about Bob's wife, Ellie, who lived in Hawaii as a child and went to Punahou. Came Pearl Harbor and she was evacuated to San Jose, where she finished high school. Her family and Bob's went to the same church and Bob's mother and brother decided that Bob was just right for her.

*A camping trip
in Europe in
1966.*

*Camping in Greece.
Bob reads Greek mythology
to the children in 1966.*

*The Parthenon,
Athens, Greece, 1966:
Carolyn, Tom, Ellie,
Mary Ellen, Bob.*

Once Bob was out of med school and Ellie completed a five-year nursing course at Stanford, they walked down the aisle on June 18, 1950, which adds up to 47 years ago.

When Bob finished his grueling internship, Ellie quietly asked, "Why don't we take a year off and travel?" Great idea, but no money.

So . . . he began working three eight-hour shifts—a regular daytime one at Kaiser's drop-in clinic, a 4 p.m. to midnight shift at Kaiser Hospital, and then on-call for emergencies from midnight to 8 a.m. Ellie worked two shifts, one as a public health nurse in San Francisco, and as a nurse in Kaiser's pediatric section. Six weeks later they had $2,000 and were off—by plane to New York, third class on the Queen Mary across the Atlantic, a cheap Left Bank hotel in Paris, where they bought a car from two Stanford boys at summer's end, and headed for Belgium.

Their budget: $2 a day, carefully nurtured, sleeping in a makeshift car bed on river banks, in hay fields, and splurging now and then in a campground in Holland, Germany, Denmark, Sweden, Norway, south to France and Spain. The cupboard was almost bare, when they heard about possible jobs at a U.S. air base near Casablanca, and ferried across the Straits of Gibraltar, to Morocco. Bob got a just-opened medic's job at the base and Ellie, with no nurse vacancies, found work in the accounting department, with the snow-covered Atlas Mountains as a backdrop.

In three months they had enough money to continue traveling. A French ship out of Marseilles took them across the Mediterranean, through the Suez, down the Red Sea, past French Somaliland in Africa to Ceylon, then to Saigon, on to Singapore and Hong Kong. Next an American freighter to Japan and then L.A., where Bob began his residency in medicine. Hard to beat or even match folks like that.

Ellie, as many know, spent 23 years at the East-West Center, a power in the population field, with several books and innumerable professional articles to her credit. She's made her own contribution to the population explosion, since she and Bob have five children, of whom they can well be proud.

Their son, who lives next door to them just above Punahou, is a physician, in charge of the Queen's Clinic in Hawaii Kai. Their four daughters include a registered nurse in Colorado, a teacher-writer living in Tokyo, an engineer-lawyer working at Hawaiian Electric Company and a registered dietitian here in Honolulu. Add to that number 11 grandchildren and you've got a good-sized voting bloc.

Bob has had a distinguished career in nuclear medicine, an impressive list of academic and hospital appointments, leadership posts in local and national organizations, and a half-dozen excellence-in-research awards. On publications, I stopped counting at 90.

Bob Nordyke lives and loves medicine, but his interests go beyond. He is a talented writer, an avid reader of such authors as Melville and Conrad, such poets as Wordsworth, T.S. Eliot, and Robert Frost, such playwrights as Eugene O'Neill, to cite but a few. He is a precise man, but a warm and compassionate and caring one who has earned widespread respect, admiration, and affection.

Five children pushed the van (with a broken generator) past the University of Moscow in the U.S.S.R. in 1970.

On a snow patch in Norway, 1970: Carolyn, Mary Ellen, Tom, Nini, Nunu.

Hiking in the Swiss Alps.

Bob and Ellie ferrying across a Norwegian fjord.

Description of Research Work Done by Robert A. Nordyke, M.D.

Dr. Robert A. Nordyke is an internationally recognized specialist in nuclear medicine and a pioneer in the field of medical informatics, recognized for his development of computerbased medical records, databases, and clinical studies of thyroid disease. Since establishing the Department of Nuclear Medicine at Straub Clinic and Hospital in 1960, Dr. Nordyke has built a uniquely large and complete thyroid disease database, which has helped uncover many new facts about these frequently underdiagnosed diseases and about their treatments. He has demonstrated the correlation between size of a goiter (thyroid gland enlargement) and increased thyroid function (hyperthyroidism), has shown how the cure rate for hypothyroidism is affected by various drug combinations and dosages, and, most recently, determined what is the most cost effective sequence of thyroid function testing for general hospital laboratory use. Dr. Nordyke developed, in collaboration with Casimir A. Kulikowski, Ph.D., one of the earliest pattern recognition methods for computer decision support employing a combination of advanced statistical and logical reasoning techniques. Dr. Nordyke's research, in collaboration with Dr. Fred Gilbert, led the research efforts on information systems for multi-specialty clinics, chronic disease clinics, and screening for breast cancer at the Pacific Health Research Institute (PHRI).

(At a time when doctors kept patient records on 3x5 index cards and were viewing the computerization of medical records with suspicion, Dr. Nordyke recognized the power of computers as tools not just for keeping tidy notes, but for gathering and analyzing medical data in a way that would help direct doctors' diagnoses and treatments for patients. A visionary always bent on improving treatment for his patients, he was 30 years ahead of his time in realizing that the kinds of patients a doctor sees vary from practice to practice and that databases collected specifically for each practice improve the quality of patient care dramatically.)

Bob Nordyke MD is a very special man, as indicated by George Chaplin, himself a very special man. Dr. Nordyke served as guest editor for the June 1995 Festschrift honoring Fred Gilbert MD—a testimonial to Fred and to his longtime associate and friend as well as to Bob. It was our largest and best Festschrift. Bob has received many accolades, accomplishments and awards—as indicated in his biography. Most recently he received a special recognition award from the Society of Nuclear Medicine, Hawaii Chapter.

Mahalo Nui Loa, Bob for the Fred Gilbert Festschrift, for your efforts to construct cabins at the YMCA Camp Erdman on Oahu's North Shore, for your years of research and administrative guidance at the Pacific Health Research Institute, for the many many patients you have helped over the years, and for your friendship.

NORMAN GOLDSTEIN, M.D.,
EDITOR, HAWAII MEDICAL JOURNAL
VOL. 56 (JULY) 1997

Robert A. Nordyke, M.D., Summarized Biography

Born:

July 14, 1919 Woodland, California

Education:

B.A., U. of California, Berkeley, in English, Public Speaking, and Political Science, 1940

M.D., U. of California, San Francisco, 1951

Rotating Internship, Kaiser Permanente Hospital, Oakland, CA, 1951–52

Residency, Internal Medicine, Wadsworth V.A. Hospital, Los Angeles, CA, 1953–56

Military Service:

U.S. Air Force, Captain, Radar Countermeasures, 1942–46

Married:

Stanford University Chapel, Stanford, June 18, 1950 to Eleanor Cole: daughter of
Louise and Ralph G. Cole (executive director of the Y.M.C.A. of the Territory
of Hawai'i, 1931–41); Punahou School, 1933–45; B.S., Stanford University, 1950;
M.P.H., U. of Hawai'i, 1969; Research Fellow, East-West Center, 1969–92;
author of *The Peopling of Hawai'i, Pacific Images.*

His Family includes:

Wife: Eleanor Cole Nordyke

Five Children: Mary Ellen Nordyke-Grace, Honolulu; Carolyn N. Cozzette,
Highlands Ranch, Colorado; Thomas A. Nordyke, M.D., Honolulu;
Gretchen (Nini) N. Worthington, Honolulu; Susan (Nunu) N. Bell,
Sunnyvale, CA

The Nordyke family in Honolulu, Hawai'i, 1981.

Thirteen Grandchildren:	Aimee M. Grace, Nalani L. Grace, Cameron N. Grace, Trevor R. Grace, Noelle W. Grace, Andrew N. Cozzette, Jennifer M. Cozzette, Larissa H. Nordyke, Veronica A. Nordyke, Thomas J. Nordyke II, Kaylin E. Worthington, Mark N. Worthington, and Baby Nordyke Bell
Three Sisters:	Betty Scher, Claremont, CA; Helen Krug, Atascadero, CA; Mary Louise Hardison, Santa Paula, CA
Brother:	James P. Nordyke, Honolulu

Certification:

Diplomate, American Board of Medical Examiners, 1959

Diplomate, American Board of Internal Medicine, 1959 and recertified 1977

Diplomate, American Board of Nuclear Medicine, 1972

Academic Appointments:

UCLA School of Medicine

Clinical Instructor, 1956–60

John A. Burns School of Medicine, University of Hawai'i

Associate Clinical Professor, Dept. of Medicine, 1966

Associate Clinical Professor, Community Health, 1974–78

Associate Professor, Dept. of Medicine, 1979–86

Chief, Div. of Nuclear Medicine, Dept. of Medicine 1978–96

Professor of Medicine, Chair of Promotion/Tenure Committee, Dept. of Medicine 1991–95

Hospital Appointments:

L.A. Veterans Administration Hospital (Wadsworth)

Assistant Chief, Radioisotope Service, 1956–60

St. Joseph's Hospital, Burbank, and St. Johns Hospital, CA.

Director, Depts. of Nuclear Medicine, 1956–60

Queen of Angels and Mt. Sinai Hospitals and Beverly Hills Clinic, CA

Consultant in Nuclear Medicine, 1956–60

UCLA Student Health Service

Radiation Safety Physician, 1958–60

Queens Hospital, Honolulu, HI

Director, Dept. of Nuclear Medicine, 1962–67

Tripler Army Hospital, Honolulu, HI

Consultant in Radioisotopes, 1960–77

Straub Clinic & Hospital, Honolulu, HI, 1960–95

Dept. of Nuclear Medicine, 1960–95

Member, Continuing Medical Education Committee, 1960–95

Co-Director, Health Appraisal Center (automated multiphasic health testing), 1968–77

   Chair, Division of Primary Care, 1972–76

   Board of Directors, 1979–85

   Co-Director, Office of Professional Activities, 1979–90

   Chair, Division of Special Services (Radiology, Pathology, Nuclear Medicine), 1980–83

   Chair, Committee on Professional Use of the Computer, 1980–83

   Chair, monthly Patient Care Conferences, 1980–92

Medical Organizations:

  American College of Physicians, 1957–97

   Fellow (FACP), 1962

   Program Chair, Annual Regional Meetings, HI, 1979, 1980

   Academic Council, 1975–95

   Governor-elect, Hawaii Chapter, 1980

   Governor, Hawaii Chapter, 1981–85

  AmericanSociety of Internal Medicine, 1960–97

   Health Care Technology Committee, 1972–75

   House of Delegates, 1980–81

   President, Hawaii Chapter, 1980–81

  Society of Nuclear Medicine (National), 1958–97

   Board of Trustees, 1962–64 and 1975–79

   President, Hawaii Chapter, 1962–63

   Academic Council, 1970–95

   Board of Directors, Western Section, 1979–80

   Credentials/Membership Committee, 1980–81

   Editorial Board, Journal of Nuclear Medicine, 1989–91

  American College of Nuclear Medicine

   Charter member, 1971

   Distinguished Fellow (FACNM), 1975

   House of Delegates, 1979–82

  American College of Nuclear Physicians

   Member, 1971–97

   Delegate from Hawaii, 1971–84

   Fellow (FACNP), 1995

   Emeritus Member, 1996

  Hawaii Medical Association

   Continuing Medical Education Program Committee, 1965–68

   Continuing Medical Education Committee, 1969–72, vice chairman, 1969

   Bureau of Research & Planning, 1971–75

   Joint Manpower Commission (physicians, nurses), 1972–75

   Chair, Health Manpower/Health Costs Committee, 1976–78

Community Health Care Committee, 1978–79

Representative to State Board of Medical Examiners, 1978

Editor of special edition of the *Hawaii Medical Journal* in honor of his colleague, Dr. Fred I. Gilbert, 1995

Honolulu County Medical Society

Delegate to HMA, 1969–74

Board of Governors, 1979–81

American Thyroid Association, 1962–97

Western Society of Clinical Research, 1958–82

American Federation of Clinical Research, 1958–95

Hawaii Academy of Science, 1962–70, Council, 1967

Pacific Health Research Institute, 1960–97

Board of Directors, 1960–91 and 1993–97

Associate Director and Secretary, 1965–85

President, 1985–91

Medical Director, 1991–95

Senior Investigator, 1995–97

Adviser to 24 summer scholars, 1960–97

Straub Pacific Health Foundation, Vice-President, 1991–93

American Board of Nuclear Medicine, Hawaii representative, 1977

National Academies of Practice, Distinguished Practitioner, Academy of Medicine, elected, 1993–97

Community Service:

University of Hawaii, Health and Social Welfare Manpower Education Council School of Medicine representative, 1972–74

Rutgers University Research Resource in Computers in Medicine. Collaborator, Expert Systems Project on Thyroid Disease (with C. Kulikowski), 1978–97

Hawaii Community Foundation Medical Advisory Committee, 1978–97

Pacific Radiopharmacy

Professional Board of Directors, 1979–95

Magnetic Resonance Imaging Advisory Board, 1983–84

Honolulu YMCA

Chairman, Camp Branch, 1964–73, Camp Erdman: instrumental in bringing about building of new cabins, other structures

Named as one of Hawaii's top doctors in *The Best Doctors in America: Pacific Region, 1996–1997* (Woodward/White Inc. of Aiken, S.C.) as reported in *Honolulu* magazine, June 1996, doctors chosen by other doctors.

Central Union Church

Outrigger Canoe Club

Awards and Publications

Awards:

First annual Professional Activities Award, Straub Clinic and Hospital, 1984

Excellence in Research Award, Straub Pacific Health Foundation, 1989–91

Laureate Award, American College of Physicians, Hawaii Chapter, 1990

Annual Koa Bowl Award, American Society of Internal Medicine, Hawaii Chapter, 1991

Excellence in Research Award, Straub Clinic and Hospital, 1991 and 1993

Excellence in Research, Arnold Award, Straub Clinic and Hospital, 1995

Special Recognition Award, Society of Nuclear Medicine, Hawaii Chapter, 1997

Publications:

Kert, M., Nordyke, R., et al.
Clinical Experiences with Reserpine (Serpasil) in Hypertension: A Preliminary Report. *Angiology* 6:138, 1955.

Pearce, M. and Nordyke, R.
Some Observations on the Effect of Heart Rate Controlled by an External Stimulator in Aortic Insufficiency. *American Journal of Medicine* 22:498, 1957.

Kert, M., Nordyke, R., et al.
Long-term Administration of Reserpine in Hypertension. *Angiology* 8:466, 1957.

Nordyke, R. and Blahd, W.
The Differential Diagnosis of Jaundice with Radioactive Rose Bengal. Second United Nations International Conference of Peaceful Uses of Atomic Energy, @/Conf. 15/876, (June) 1958.

Nordyke, R. and Pearce. M.
Renal Adaptations to Postural Changes in Chronic Congestive Heart Failure. *American Heart Journal* 56:202, 1958.

Kert, M., Nordyke, R., et al.
Clinical Evaluation of Chlorisondamine (Ecolid) in the Treatment of Hypertension. *Angiology* 9:303, 1958.

Nordyke, R.
Differential Diagnosis of Biliary Tract Obstruction with Radioiodinated Rose Bengal. *Clinical Research Proceedings* 7:2, 295, 1959.

Nordyke, R. and Blahd, W.
Blood Disappearance of Radioactive Rose Bengal: Rapid Simple Test of Liver Function. *Journal of the American Medical Association* 170:1159, 1959.

Nordyke, R., Tubis, M. and Blahd, W.
Simultaneous Comparison of Individual Kidney Function Using Radioiodinated Hippuran. *Clinical Research Proceedings* 8:203, (January) 1960.

Matthews, R., Tubis, M., Blahd, W. and Nordyke,R.
A Comparison of Radioiodinated BSP with Radioiodinated Rose Bengal in Humans. *Clinical Research Proceedings* 8:203, (January) 1960.

Oldendorf, W., Crandall, P., Nordyke, R. and Rose, A.
A Comparison of the Arrival in the Cerebral Hemispheres of Intravenously Injected Radioisotope. *Neurology* 10:223, (March) 1960.

Tubis, M., Posnick, E. and Nordyke, R.
Preparation and Use of I-131 Labeled Sodium Iodohippurate in Kidney Function Tests. *Proceedings of the Society of Experimental Biology and Medicine* 103:497, (March) 1960.

Nordyke, R.
The Radioisotope Renogram: Advances in Test Agent and Instrumentation. *Journal of Nuclear Medicine* 1:125, (April) 1960.

Nordyke, R.
Biliary Tract Obstruction and its Localization with Radioiodinated Rose Bengal. *American Journal of Gastroenterology* 33:563, (May) 1960.

Tubis, M., Blahd, W., and Nordyke, R.
The Preparation.and Use of Radioiodinated Congo Red in Detecting Amyloidosis. *Journal of the American Pharmaceutical Association* (Scientific Ed.) 49:422, (July) 1960.

Blahd, W., Nordyke, R. and Bauer, F.
Radioactive Iodine (I-131) in the Postoperative
Treatment of Thyroid Cancer. *Cancer* 13:745,
(July–August) 1960.

Nordyke, R.
Radioiodinated Rose Bengal in Liver
and Biliary Tract Function Testing. A
Reappraisal. *Gastroenterology* 39:258,
(August) 1960.

Nordyke, R., Tubis, M. and Blahd, W.
The Use of Radioiodinated Hippuran for
Individual Kidney Function Testing. *Journal
of Laboratory and Clinical Medicine* 60:438,
(September) 1960.

Tubis, M., Blahd, W. and Nordyke, R.
Developments in the Use of Hippuran in
the Radioisotope Renogram. *USVA Annual
Research Conference Bulletin*, (November)
1960.

Nordyke, R. and Blahd, W.
Liver and Biliary Tract Function Testing
with Radioiodinated Rose Bengal. *Journal
of Wadsworth General Hospital* 4:167,
(December) 1960.

Winter, C. C., Nordyke, R. and Tubis, M.
Clinical Experience with a New Test Agent
for the Radioisotope Renogram: Sodium
Ortho-Iodohippurate-I-131 (Hippuran I-131).
Journal of Urology 85:92 (January) 1961.

Nordyke, R.
Biliary Tract Obstruction Demonstrated
by Radioactive Rose Bengal: Studies of
116 Consecutive Jaundiced Patients.
Clinical Research 9:89, (January) 1961.

Rigler, R. G., Nordyke, R. and
Gilbert, F. I., Jr.
Radioiodine Treatment of Hyperthyroidism.
Hawaii Medical Journal 20:466, (May–June)
1961.

Nordyke, R.
Renal Artery Obstruction. *Lancet*,
(June 3) 1961, p. 1226.

Nordyke, R.
Individual Kidney Function Testing with
Radioactive Tracers. *Proceedings for the
Hawaii Academy of Science 36th Annual
Meeting Abstracts*, 1960–61.

Rufin, F., Blahd, W., Nordyke, R. and
Grossman, M.
Reliability of I^{131} Triolein Test in the
Detection of Steatorrhea. *Gastroenterology*
41:220, (September) 1961.

Nordyke, R.
Pituitary-Adrenal Suppression and
Stimulation Tests. *Straub Clinic Proceedings*
27:135, (September) 1961.

Nordyke, R.
Some Background Comments of Steroids.
Straub Clinic Proceedings 27:124, (August)
1961.

Tubis M., Nordyke, R., Posnick, E. and
Blahd, W.
The Preparation and Use of I^{131} Labeled
Sulfobromophthalein in Liver Function
Testing. *Journal of Nuclear Medicine* 2:282,
(October) 1961.

Nordyke, R.
Liver and Biliary Tract Function Testing with
Radioiodinated Rose Bengal. *Hawaii Medical
Journal* 21:144, (November–December) 1961.

Nordyke, R.
The Radioisotope Renogram: Advance in
Test Substance and Procedure. *Journal of
Nuclear Medicine* 3:67, (January) 1962.

Nordyke, R.
Tests for Small-Bowel Function
(Radioisotopes). In *The CIBA Collection of
Medical Illustrations*. Netter. Vol 3 Digestive
Systems, 1962.

Nordyke, R. and Tonchen, A.
A Comparison of Thyroid Function Tests:
The 6 and 24-hour Thyroidal Uptake, T-3
Red Cell Uptake, T-3 Resin Uptake, Reflex
Recording and the PBI. *Journal of Nuclear
Medicine* 3:218, (May) 1962.

Nordyke, R.
The Radiohippuran Renogram: Enhanced
Reproducibility by Changes in Collimation,
Kidney-Crystal Distance, and Patient
Position. *Journal of Nuclear Medicine*
3:218 (May) 1962.

Nordyke, R., Rigler, R. G. and Strode, W. S.
Radioisotope Renography: Current Status
and Simplified Procedure. *American Journal
of Roentgenology Radiation Therapy & Nuclear
Medicine* 88:311, (August) 1962.

Nordyke, R. and Tonchen, A.
The Radiohippuran Renogram.
JAMA 183:144, February 9, 1963.

West, R. and Nordyke, R.
The Use of the Renogram in Obstetrics
and Gynecology. *Western Journal of Surgery,
Obstetrics and Gynecology* 71:1, (January–
February) 1963.

Brault, A. and Nordyke, R.
Screening of 400 Unselected Hypertensive Patients for Unilateral Kidney Disease, Preliminary Report. *Straub Clinic Proceedings* 29:52, (April) 1963.

Nordyke, R.
Renograms. *British Medical Journal,* May 11, 1963, p. 1288.

Nordyke, R.
The Overactive and Underactive Thyroid. *American Journal of Nursing* 63, (May) 1963.

Brault, A. and Nordyke R.
Screening of Unselected Hypertension Patients with Radiorenography. *Clinical Research* 12:121, (January) 1964.

Nordyke, R.
Radioisotope Renography. Chapter in Blahd, W. H. (Ed.), *Nuclear Medicine,* McGraw-Hill, 1965.

Nordyke, R.
Surgical vs. Non-Surgical Jaundice: Differentiation by a Combination of Rose Bengal 1^{131} and Standard Liver-Function Tests. *JAMA* 194:949, (November) 1965.

Nordyke, R.
Screening for Thyroxicosis by the Achilles' Reflex Time. *Pacific Medicine & Surgery* 74:8, 1966 (also *Clinical Research* 13:246, April, 1966).

Nordyke, R.
The Cause of Hyperthyroidism in Graves' Disease. *Straub Clinic Proceedings,* (January–March) 1966, p. 3.

Okihiro, M. and Nordyke, R.
Hypokalemic Periodic Paralysis; Experimental Precipitation with L-Triiodothyronine. *JAMA* 198:949, November 21, 1966.

Nordyke, R. and Gilbert, F. I., Jr.
Mass Screening for Hypothyroidism by the Achilles' Reflex Time. *Archives of Environmental Health* 14:827, 1967, (also, *Clinical Research* 15:125, 1967).

Gilbert, F. I., Jr. and Nordyke, R.
Periodic Examination of the Apparently Well Individual. *The International Conference on Medical & Biological Engineering.* Stockholm, 1967, p. 178.

Nordyke R., Gilbert, F. I., Jr. and Simmons, E. L.
Screening for Kidney Disease with Radioisotopes. *JAMA* 208:493, April 21, 1969.

Nordyke, R. A. and Worth, R. M.
The Prevalence of Hypothyroidism and Hyperthyroidism in a Random Sample of Civilian Residents of Oahu: Description of a Study. *Chronic Disease Newsletter,* Hawaii State Department of Health #10, December, 1969.

Nordyke, R.
Long-term Follow-up of Patients Treated for Thyrotoxicosis Using the Achilles' Reflex Time. *Hormones* 1:36–45, 1970.

Nordyke, R. and Freeman, G.
Post-Treatment Hypothyroidism: Simplified Detection and Follow-up System Using the Achilles' Reflex Time. *Surgical Clinics of North America* 50:319–327, (April) 1970.

Nordyke, R. and Gilbert, F. I., Jr.
The Achilles' Reflex Thyroid Function Test: Evaluation of a New Instrument. *American Journal of the Medical Sciences* 259:419–4232, (June) 1970.

Nordyke, R., Kulikowski, C. A. and Kulikowski, C. W.
A Comparison of Methods for the Automated Diagnosis of Thyroid Dysfunction. *Computers and Biomedical Research* 4:374, 1971.

Nordyke, R.
Radioisotope Renography, Chapter in Blahd, W. H. (Ed.) 2nd Edition, *Nuclear Medicine,* McGraw-Hill, 1971.

Levin, M. H., Nordyke, R. and Gall, J. J.
Demonstration of Dissecting Popliteal Cyst by Joint Scans After Intra-articular Isotope Injections. *Arthritis and Rheumatism* 14:591–598, (September–October) 1971.

Nordyke, R.
Screening for Thyroid Disease by use of Allied Health Personnel and Computer Analysis. *Proceedings of the 5th Hawaii International Conference of Systems Sciences.* Computers in Biomedicine, 1972. Western Periodicals.

Ball, J., Nordyke, R. and Kistner, R.
Pulmonary Embolism in Deep Leg Vein Thrombosis. *Hawaii Medical Journal* 31:101, (March–April) 1972.

Nordyke, R.
Metabolic and Physiologic Aspects of 131-1 Rose Bengal in Studying Liver Function. *Seminars in Nuclear Medicine* 2:157–166, (April) 1972. Also published in *Radionuclide Studies of the Gastrointestinal System*, (Eds) Freeman, L. M. and Blaufox, M. D., Grune and Stratton, New York & London, 1973. Also published in *Medicine Nucleare*, 3:201–14, December 1973.

Kistner, R. L., Ball, J. J., Nordyke, R. and Freeman, G. C.
Incidence of Pulmonary Embolism in the Course of Thrombophlebitis of the Lower Extremities. *American Journal of Surgery* 124:169–176, (August) 1972.

Nordyke, R.
The Computer in Medicine. Symposium Introduction, *Straub Clinic Proceedings*, (April–June) 1972.

Nordyke, R.
Computers in Office Practice—A Thyroid Model. *Straub Clinic Proceedings*, (April–June) 1972, p. 53.

Gilbert, F. I., Jr. and Nordyke, R.
Automated Multiphasic Health Testing in a Multiple Specialty Group Practice. *Preventive Medicine* 1:261–265, (June) 1973.

Zimmerman, H. J., Nordyke, R., et al.
Forum: Surgical Jaundice. Differentiation by Radiologic Techniques. *Modern Medicine* 41:68, November 26, 1973.

Nordyke, R.
Therapeutic Trial for Hypothyroidism. *Clinical Research* 22:165A, (February) 1974.

Nordyke, R.
Definition and Goals of Primary Care. In *Advances in Primary Care*. Ed. Kallstrom and Yarnall, (February) 1974.

Nordyke, R.
The Use of Radioisotopes in Biliary Tract Diagnosis: An Overview. *Bordeaux Medical* 16:1291, (June) 1976.

Nordyke, R.
Experiences with A Protocol for Thyroid Disorders. In *Design and Use of Protocols. Advances in Patient Care*. Eds. Kallstrom and Yarnall, (February) 1975, p. 125.

Moreno-Cabral, R., Kistner, R. L. and Nordyke, R.
Importance of Calf Vein Thrombophlebitis. *Surgery* 80:735–742, (December) 1976.

Nordyke, R. and Gilbert, F. I., Jr.
Share-care Clinics. In *The Changing Health Care Team*, 1976, p. 72, published by Medical Communications and Services Association, Seattle, Washington.

Gilbert, F. I., Jr. and Nordyke, R.
Sequential Radionuclide Venography and Lung Scans in the Diagnosis of Venous Thrombi and Pulmonary Emboli. *Straub Clinic Proceedings* 45:18–21, 1980.

O'Leary, M. J., Limpisvasti, P., Nordyke, R. and Kistner, R. L.
Massive Thrombosis in Systemic Lupus Erythematosus. *Hawaii Medical Journal* 39:81, 1980.

Nordyke, R., Nordyke, T. J. and Kulikowski, C. A.
The Diagnosis of Decompensated Hypothyroidism by a Therapeutic Trial with Thyroid Hormones. *American Thyroid Association, Supplement to Endocrinology*, 19:T-48, (September) 1981.

Fitz-Patrick, D., DeSilva, A. C. and Nordyke, R.
An Unusual Case of Hyperthyroxinemia. *Straub Clinic Proceedings* 47:12–13, (December) 1982.

Brady, S. K. and Nordyke, R.
Computer Aided Diagnosis of Pulmonary Embolism. *Straub Clinic Proceedings* 49:64–70, (August) 1984.

Gilbert, F. I., Jr., Nordyke, R., Catts, A., Russell, H. and Balfour, J.
Screening for Breast Cancer in Hawaii. Review of the first 100 cases found.

Moreno-Cabral, R. J., Kong, A., Lindberg, R., Nordyke, R. and Kistner, R. L.
The Value of Prophylactic Heparin Following Hip Fractures.

Nordyke, R., Gilbert, F. I., Jr. and Harada, A.S.M.
Correlation Between Goiter Size and the Degree of Hyperthyroidism in Graves Disease. *Straub Proceedings* 51:16–18, (July) 1986. Summary published in *Clinical Research* 34:431A (April) 1986.

Nordyke, R., Gilbert, F. I., Jr. and Miyamoto, L.
Management of Primary Hypothyroidism Using a Sensitive TSH Assay. *Postgraduate Medicine* 80 (4):145–9, (September) 1986. Also published in *Clinical Research* 34:430A, 1986.

Nordyke, R. and Gilbert, F. I., Jr.
The Achilles Reflex Time in the Diagnosis of Hyperthyroidism. *Clinical Research* 34:431A, (April) 1986.

Nordyke, R., Gilbert, F.I. Jr., and
Harada, A.S.M.
  Graves' Disease: Influence of Age on
  Clinical Findings. *Arch Int Medicine*
  148:626–31, (March) 1988.
Nordyke, R. and Gilbert F. I., Jr.
  Using the Computer in the Doctor's Office
  to Enhance Quality of Patient Care. *The
  Straub Foundation Proceedings* 55:17–21,
  (August) 1990.
Nordyke, R., and Gilbert, F. I., Jr.
  Management of Primary Hypothyroidism.
  Comprehensive Therapy 16:28–32, (July) 1990.
Nordyke, R., Gilbert, F. I., Jr. and Wu, H. M.
  Treatment of Hypothyroidism: Dose and
  Follow-up Time Intervals. *The Straub Foun-
  dation Proceedings* 55:35–36 (November) 1990.
Nordyke, R. and Gilbert, F. I., Jr.
  Optimal Iodine 131 Dose for Eliminating
  Hyperthyroidism in Graves' Disease. *J Nucl
  Med* 32:411–416, (March) 1991. Also, summary
  in Endocrinology Vol. 122, Supplement,
  p. T-12, 1989.
Nordyke, R., Gilbert, F. I., Jr. and Lew, C.
  Painful Subacute Thyroiditis in Hawaii:
  Clinical Features and Natural History.
  Western J Med 155:61–63 (July) 1991.
Nordyke, R. and Gilbert, F. I., Jr.
  Eliminating Hyperthyroidism. (Letter)
  J Nucl Med 32:1642 (August) 1991.

Nordyke, R. and Gilbert, F. I., Jr.
  Optimal Iodine-131 Dose in Graves' Disease
  (Letter) *J Nucl Med* 32:2360 (December) 1991.
Gilbert, F. I., Jr. and Nordyke, R. A.
  The Case for Restructuring Health Care in
  the United States: The Hawaii Paradigm.
  J Med Systems August, 1993; 17:283–288.
Nordyke, R. A., Gilbert, F.I., Jr.,
Miyamoto, L. A., Fleury, K. A.
  The Superiority of Antimicrosomal Over
  Antithyroglobulin Antibodies for Detecting
  Hashimoto's Thyroiditis. *Arch Int Med* April,
  1993; 153:862–865.
Nordyke, R. A.
  Hawaii Med Journal. June. 1995. Issue Editor.
  Introductions, memorial statement to Fred I.
  Gilbert, M.D., editorial comments through-
  out issue.
Nordyke, R. A., Reppun T. S., Woods, J. C.,
Goldstein, A. P., Miyamoto, L. A.,
Madanay, L. D.
  Alternative Sequences of TSH and FT4 in
  Routine Thyroid Function Testing: Quality
  and Cost. *Arch Intern Med*, Feb., 1998.
Nordyke, R. A. and Kulikowski, C. A.
  An Informatics-based Chronic Disease
  Practice: Case Study of a 35-year Computer-
  based Longitudinal Record System.
  J Am Medical Informatics Association,
  Vol. 5, No. 1:88–103, Jan./Feb. 1998.

*Straub Clinic and Hospital's Excellence in Research
award was presented to Robert A. Nordyke, M.D.
and Fred I. Gilbert, Jr., M.D. in 1991 and 1993.
Dr. Sada Okumura (above center) congratulates
the recipients in 1991.*

❧ *Remembrances of Robert A. Nordyke, M.D.* ❧

In March, 1997 Bob Nordyke felt a slight abdominal discomfort. A battery of tests revealed adenocarcinoma of the esophagus and upper stomach with metastases. The fast-growing cancer invaded and took his life on August 23, 1997. Husband, father, brother, grandfather, physician, friend—Bob touched and healed thousands. Some said, "Bob was a saint in our world!" The *Honolulu Advertiser* called him "a treasure of Hawaii."

These are some of the descriptions of this remarkable man that were received in beautiful letters of remembrance:

- Quiet and gentle
- Sincere
- Thoughtful
- Gracious
- Sense of humor
- Selfless
- Loving and kind
- Sensitive
- Ahead of his time
- Integrity and fairness
- Brilliant
- Humility
- Intellectual drive
- Compassion
- A habit of excellence
- Cheerful
- An inspiration
- Friendly, warm, and giving
- A valued researcher
- Unassuming
- Willing and enthusiastic
- Understanding
- Kind-spirited
- Creative
- Humble
- Never derogatory
- Caring
- Devotion to family

- Honest
- Concern for others
- My guardian angel
- Futurist and visionary
- A keen searching mind
- Personal discipline
- A spirit of exploration
- Zest for life
- An exceptional and wonderful human being.
- A guiding force and the calm voice of reason.
- A wonderful example of a life of fullness and dedication to humanity.
- An extraordinary person, not only by the depth of his understanding and sensitivity, but also in the breadth of his insights.
- A legacy of excellence in medicine and the shining example of a true Christian gentleman.
- A role model for sharing knowledge, mentoring, and high ethical standards.
- Modest in professional brilliance, understated in numerous achievements, generous to a fault; a rare individual who grasped life fully and surely and made it all look easy.

Nordyke was one of our treasures

By George Chaplin

Voltaire said: "Men who are occupied in the restoration of health to other men, by the joint exertion of skill and humanity, are above all the great of the earth. They even partake of divinity, since to preserve and renew is almost as noble as to create."

Many of Hawaii's physicians merit such an encomium, but none more than the late Dr. Robert Nordyke.

He is well recognized as a pioneer in nuclear medicine, but how many know his background, his formative years that made him into the multi-faceted person that he was?

He arrived 78 years ago in a California farming town, Woodland, in the Sacramento Valley, a town so small the kids could walk to either the elementary or the high school. It was a time of screened porches and rocking chairs, a time of basic American values. His was a family with little money, but with seven children and lots of love — as well as a tree house that could be reached by climbing out of a second-story window and jumping from the roof.

10 cents an hour

One summer during the Depression, he picked apricots on a ranch just out of town. He worked 10 hours a day, at 10 cents an hour, with 10 cents deducted for a sandwich and flavored water. Lunch! Incidentally, 10 cents is what it took in those days for a Saturday matinee featuring Tom Mix or Hoot Gibson.

Bob was graduated from Berkeley in 1940, having majored in English literature, political science and public speaking.

He signed up with his draft board, and followed with a two-month course in San Francisco in radio repair and radio telegraphy. He then thumbed his way to San

Robert Nordyke

Diego and got a job as radio operator on a large tuna fishing boat manned by Portuguese, only three of whom spoke any English.

Came the war and Captain Robert Allan Nordyke put in four years in radar countermeasures. Next, med school at the University of California, San Francisco, on the GI Bill. But there was no money to pay for the mortgage on a house he and brother Jim, a Navy lieutenant fresh from service, bought for their mother and themselves in Berkeley.

1928 Chevy

So he and Jim bought a 1928 Chevy with a flat bed for $75 and went into the trash-hauling business in between classes. They did well and soon graduated to a 1½-ton surplus army truck bought at an auction.

Five years later, when interning at the Kaiser Permanente Hospital in Oakland, Bob Nordyke delivered, under supervision, 80 babies in a single month. Near the end of that rotation, at one delivery, he took off his mask and looked up at the new mother from between her draped legs and told her that all was well and that she had a beautiful baby.

She looked him straight in the eye and then, puzzled and upset, she said:

"Aren't you my trash man?"

Bob's wife, Ellie, lived in Hawaii as a child and went to Punahou. Came Pearl

Harbor and she was evacuated to San Jose, where she finished high school. Her family and Bob's went to the same church and Bob's mother and brother decided that Bob was just right for her.

Once Bob was out of med school and Ellie completed a five-year nursing course at Stanford, they walked down the aisle on June 18, 1950, 47 years ago.

Once Bob finished his grueling internship, Ellie quietly asked: "Why don't we take a year off and travel?" Great idea, but no money.

So . . . he began working three eight-hour shifts — a regular daytime shift at Kaiser's drop-in clinic, a 4 p.m. to midnight shift at Kaiser Hospital, and then was on call for emergencies from midnight to 8 a.m. Ellie worked two shifts, one as a public health nurse in San Francisco and the other as a nurse in Kaiser's pediatric section.

Off to see the world

Six weeks later they had $2,000 and were off — by plane to New York, third class on the Queen Mary across the Atlantic, a cheap Left Bank hotel in Paris, where they bought a car from two Stanford boys at summer's end, and headed for Belgium.

Their budget: $2 a day, carefully nurtured, sleeping in a makeshift car bed on river banks, in hay fields,

and splurging now and then in a campground. Holland, Germany, Denmark, Sweden, Norway, south to France and Spain. The cupboard was almost bare, when they heard about possible jobs at a U.S. air base near Casablanca, and headed there.

In three months they had enough money to continue traveling: A French ship out of Marseilles took them across the Mediterranean, through the Suez down the Red Sea, past French Somali land in Africa to Ceylon, then to Saigon, on to Singapore and Hong Kong. Next an American freighter to Japan and then L.A., where Bob began his residency in medicine. Hard to beat or even match folks like that.

Ellie, as many know, spent 23 years at the East-West Center, a power in the population field, with several books and innumerable professional articles to her credit. She and Bob raised five fine children.

Five children

Their son, who lives next door to his parents' home just above Punahou, is a physician, in charge of the Queen's Clinic in Hawaii Kai. Their four daughters include a registered nurse in Colorado, a teacher-writer living in Tokyo, an engineer-lawyer and a teacher-registered dietitian here. Add 11 grandchildren and you've got a good-sized voting bloc.

Bob had a distinguished career in nuclear medicine, an impressive list of academic and hospital appointments, leadership posts in local and national organizations, and a half-dozen excellence-in-research awards. On publications, I stopped counting at 90.

Bob Nordyke lived and loved medicine, but his interests went beyond. He was a talented writer, an avid reader of such authors as Melville and Conrad, such poets as Wordsworth, T.S. Eliot, and Robert Frost, such playwrights as Eugene O'Neill, to cite but a few. He was a precise man, but a warm and compassionate and caring one who earned widespread respect, admiration and affection.

George Chaplin, retired editor of The Advertiser, is now editor at large.

Nordyke's career

Pioneer in nuclear medicine, computerized medicine, and what is now known as medical informatics; superb clinician, widely published medical researcher, medical educator, innovative administrator. Straub Clinic and Hospital, pacific Health and Research Institute and Straub Pacific Health Foundation. Professor of Medicine at John A. Burns School of Medicine, 1991- 1995. Named as one of Hawaii's top doctors in The Best Doctors in America: Pacific Region, 1996-97 (Woodward/White Inc. of Aiken, S.C.) as reported in Honolulu magazine, June 1996, doctors chosen by other doctors.

— George Chaplin

From The Honolulu Advertiser, *August 31, 1997*

Bob opens a birthday present with the help of his grandchildren,
Nalani, Cameron, Trevor, and Aimee Grace on July 14, 1991

- The 'true gentleman' of Hawai'i.
- A pioneer in the development of the American College of Physicians in Hawai'i.
- The creative, visionary member of the group. I remember my husband coming home thirty-five years ago, all excited about what Bob was doing with computers and the revolutionary effects they would have on medicine.
- My *most-admired* physician and person. I will never forget him.
- A highly talented physician as well as an empathetic one. The two traits don't often go hand-in-hand.
- An outstanding citizen, wonderful YMCA leader and supporter, a life of service to others.
- One of the finest men I ever knew.
- His life represents the very best a human can offer. We have been so fortunate to share it.
- His life encompassed the word "graciousness." He never had an unkind word to say about anyone, he rarely showed impatience or anger, he trusted people and gave everyone the benefit of the doubt, he was honest and expected the truth in return, he defined good manners and was unassuming in all his accomplishments.
- He had my utmost respect; it was a privilege to work with him.
- He possessed a unique ability to listen to you in a thoughtful and uncritical manner, giving you the focus of all his attention that made you feel truly special.
- Bob was always very kind. He was never too busy for you. When I would come to his office, he would stop his work to greet me, and he made me feel so welcome and special.

- He has always been a model for the way a professional should act: intelligent, modest, and kind. Because of Bob, I've been a better teacher, holding my tongue and making allowances for student learning. In a word, I've become a better person for having known him.
- It was to Bob that I turned for advice; yet in my many years of practice in Hawai'i, he was the only nuclear medical physician to call and ask me how to interpret a special problem. Such humility is the true mark of greatness, and in my opinion, Bob was one of those truly great physicians and men.
- This gentle man embodied the highest and best in our professional ideals, always teaching and learning, with a habit of excellence in all he did.
- He was my hero and an irreplaceable friend.
- He was always reading, studying, analyzing. He stayed at the forefront of the medical field and pushed the limits of medical knowledge.

- A scholar with a great command of the English language, poetry, and literature. I was constantly impressed by the clarity and beauty of his words.
- He authored over 100 scientific articles; two research papers to be published soon were written during his illness.
- He placed love, knowledge, and nature above material possessions.
- He pointed out the wonders of life—the stars, the birds, the trees, the mountains, the paintings, sculptures, and poetry.
- Some people are special in a few realms of understanding; Bob was special in every aspect of life.
- What an inspiration Bob is! His writings show such enjoyable humor and insight! His gracious letters to my mother put a sparkle in her eyes and gratefulness in her heart!
- I remember vividly my first meeting with Bob. He came through to me in an absolutely clear way that has remained unchanged over many decades, clear and strong as though it were captured in a painting. He is simply unforgettable.
- I saw so much kindness and concern for others in his eyes.

- We felt in awe of his brilliance, his talent with music, and his ability to be an incredible family man.
- You'll never know how many patients share in the loss of this gentle and caring man.
- He told me that I was a *very young* 80! I've been in love with him ever since!
- My daughter had thyroid cancer. His expertise made her well. She thought the world of him.
- I loved him from the first moment I saw him, and every day and every hour since then—I love him. He was a fine man whom everyone loved and admired, and so beautiful in mind and heart.
- He soothed my fears and helped me feel better so many countless times throughout my life. He was always there for me.
- He was so warm and welcoming, opening his home to so many.
- [From a daughter] As busy as Dad was with his medical work, he made it a priority to take us on extended camping trips to many parts of the world, because he knew it would help us understand and respect different cultures and ideas.
- [From a daughter] He told us: "Wherever you are, be all there!" and "If you say you will do something, do it completely, without complaint, and with optimism."
- You could tell that he was proud of his wife and each member of his family.
- I've used Bob's devotion to family and Ellie's valuing of family life to slow us and cherish what we have.
- I always loved seeing you two together. There was a unique joy and spark of energy.
- [From a daughter] We grew up seeing how proud Dad and Mom were of each other's accomplishments, how accepting and understanding they were of each other, how happy they were to see each other at the end of every day, how comfortable they were together. Marriage doesn't get better than that.
- It was everyone's idea of the perfect couple: there was warmth, sincerity, and strength of character.
- [From a granddaughter] I have lately truly realized but inside always known just what an exceptional man my Grandpa was—a wealth of knowledge, well-rounded, caring, supportive, encouraging, sweet, and always there to help. He loved music, and I'll miss his cello, harmonizing, and singing at family gatherings. He grew up in the Depression when money was scarce, and he taught us that "Pleasure comes from less, rather than excess!" and poems like William Wordsworth's "The world is too much with us; late and soon, getting and spending, we lay waste our powers; little we see in nature that is ours; we have given our lives away—." I eagerly spent the night at Gramma and Grandpa's home, staying up late to listen to Grampa's wonderful stories, like riding on top of railroad cars to go to fight fires in Montana, the effects of the Depression on his father's farm, hauling trash to earn money to go to medical school, the dozen roses for Gramma on every anniversary, his mother who was a

schoolteacher, and his grandmother who crossed the country in a covered wagon. I loved to hear and recite some special selections from his marvelous world of poetry. John Donne's poem "No man is an island" symbolized Grandpa's feelings that we are all interconnected by a common bond. I know you are here in each of us, Grandpa. Thank you for so enriching our lives.

♦ Bob has had a remarkable impact on families, our community, and the medical profession. He has ennobled us all.

♦ He never complained or expressed self-pity. He made an effort to reduce the emotional impact of his illness, and a visit with him left us uplifted.

♦ After the beautiful memorial service for Bob, as we drove over the Pali, we were met with a gentle misty rain and the most perfectly formed and vividly colored rainbow— a tribute to our dear friend.

♦ You are a special star to pass through this earth. Where is your next destination?

♦ If all of us could emulate Bob Nordyke in our day-to-day lives and pass on his outstanding qualities to our fellow men, the world would be a much better place.

♦ [From his wife] As Bob slipped away from this life, with family and friends at his hospital bedside, his very last spoken words were "I love you."

References

Bartlett, John, ed. 1944. *Familiar Quotations*. Garden City, N.Y.: Garden City Publishing Co.

"A blast from the past for Dingle School," *Woodland (Calif.) Daily Democrat*, Nov. 5, 1993, A-5.

Book of Knowledge, The Children's Encyclopedia. New York: The Grolier Society. 1922.

Bowen, Ezra. 1972. *The High Sierra*. New York: Time-Life Books: 18–19, 116–117.

Braddy, Nella, ed. 1932. *The Standard Book of British and American Verse*. Garden City, N.Y.: Garden City Publishing Co.

Cather, Willa. 1926. *My Antonia*. Boston: Houghton Mifflin Co.

Chaplin, George. Commentary. *Hawaii Medical Journal*, 56 (1997): 168–172.

Conley, Cort [text], and John Marshall [photography]. 1997. *Idaho*. Portland, Oreg.: Graphic Arts Center Publishing Co.: 87.

Conrad, Joseph. 1900. *Lord Jim*. Edinburgh: William Blackwood and Sons.

Curtis, Charles P. Jr., and Ferris Greenslet. 1962. *The Practical Cogitator*. Boston: Houghton Mifflin Co.

Fleming, Thomas C. *The Free Press: Reflections on Black History*. Riding the Freights. Part 50. 1998.

Frost, Robert. 1942. *Collected Poems of Robert Frost*. Garden City, N.Y.: Halcyon House.

GEO Expeditions. 1996. *Galapagos Islands, 1996 & 1997*. Sonora, Calif.

Hamsun, Knut. 1921. *Growth of the Soil*. Translated by W.W. Worster. New York: Alfred A. Knopf.

Hogan, Elizabeth, ed. 1977. *Beautiful California*. Menlo Park, Calif.: Sunset Books, Lane Publishing Co.: 7–9.

Horace [Quintus Horatius Flaccus]. 65–68 B.C. *Book II Ode X*. "If Hindrances Obstruct Thy Way," translated by William Cowper, in Bartlett 1944: 267.

Kilmer, Fred B. 1916. *Household Handbook. Suggestions for the Prevention of the Spread of Disease and the Care of the Sick*. New Brunswick, N.J.: 10.

Larkey, Joann L., and Shipley Walters. 1987. *Yolo County—Land of Changing Patterns*. Woodland, Calif.: Windsor Publications: 66, 109.

Leffingwell, Randy. 1997. *Caterpillar Dozers and Tractors*. Ann Arbor, Mich.: Lowe & B. Hould, Publishers: 22.

Lott, Milton J. 1954. *The Last Hunt*. Boston: Houghton Mifflin Co.

Melville, Herman. 1930. *Moby Dick*. Chicago: Lakeside Press.

Milosz, Czeslaw. 1968. *Native Realm: A Search for Self-Definition*. Translated by Catherine S. Leach. Berkeley: University of California Press: 20.

Nordyke, Eleanor C., and Aimee M. Grace, eds. 1999. *A Gathering of Flowers: One Man's Anthology*, Favorite Poems and Selections of Robert A. Nordyke. Honolulu, Hawai'i: private printing.

Page, Curtis H., ed. 1904. *British Poets of the Nineteenth Century.* New York: Benjamin H. Sanborn & Co.

Pinegar, Ron, and David Wilkinson. 1997. *The Walking Tour of Historic Woodland.* Woodland, Calif.: Historical Preservation Commission and City of Woodland Council.

"Program Told for Town, Country Club Guest Afternoon." *Woodland (Calif.) Daily Democrat,* 9 October 1934.

"The United States," National Geographic Magazine. 1991.

"Woodland Boy Works Way Through Mills College." *Woodland (Calif.) Daily Democrat,* 10 June 1935.

Index